UNLOCKING
the SECRETS
OF THE FEASTS

Published in Nashville, Tennessee, by WestBow Press, an imprint of Thomas Nelson. WestBow Press and Thomas Nelson are registered trademarks of HarperCollins Christian Publishing, Inc.

Unless otherwise indicated, scripture quotations taken from the New American Standard Bible®, Copyright © 1960, 1962, 1963, 1968, 1971, 1972, 1973, 1975, 1977, 1995 by The Lockman Foundation. Used by permission. (www.Lockman.org)

Thomas Nelson, Inc. titles may be purchased in bulk for educational, business, fund-raising, or sales promotional use. For information, please e-mail SpecialMarkets@ThomasNelson.com.

Because of the dynamic nature of the Internet, any web addresses or links contained in this book might have changed since publication and may no longer be valid. The views expressed in this work are solely those of the author and do not necessarily reflect the views of the publisher, and the publisher hereby disclaims any responsibility for them.

Any people depicted in stock imagery provided by Thinkstock are models, and such images are being used for illustrative purposes only.

Certain stock imagery © Thinkstock.

Library of Congress Control Number: 2011962733

ISBN: 9780718037024 (sc)
ISBN: 9780718037031 (e)

Printed in the United States of America
HB 08.22.2023

UNLOCKING
the SECRETS
OF THE FEASTS

The Prophecies *in the* Feasts *of* Leviticus

MICHAEL NORTEN

WESTBOW
PRESS

An Imprint of Thomas Nelson
visit us at: thomasnelson.com

To the memory of my mother, Nadine Norten,
who was very interested in the subject of the
feasts of Leviticus and Bible prophecy.

CONTENTS

Acknowledgments   ix
Preface   xi
Introduction   xv

One
The Passover   1

Two
The Feast of Unleavened Bread   15

Three
The Feast of Firstfruits   25

Four
The Feast of Pentecost   35

Five
The Feast of Trumpets   43

Six
The Day of Atonement   55

Seven
The Feast of Tabernacles   67

Conclusion   83
Bibliography   87
About the Author   89

ACKNOWLEDGMENTS

I am very grateful to the late Dr. Roy Zuck, former senior professor at Dallas Theological Seminary, for the initial editing of the text, and Dr. John Reed, senior professor emeritus of pastoral ministries at Dallas Theological Seminary, for his advice and encouragement. I am also immensely grateful for the additional encouragement provided by my wife, Ann.

PREFACE

When I was a college student, I took advantage of an opportunity during the Christmas holiday to take a train ride to Mexico City with a number of other students. Some people warned me that desperadoes liked to rob people on trains in Mexico, so I needed to be on guard. Obviously for a young college student, that piece of information caused a great deal of imagination and concern. But by the time I was on the train, leaving Laredo, Texas, my concerns were mostly replaced by excitement and adventure.

The train ride took two very long days to get all the way to Mexico City, so by the second day those warnings began to weigh on my mind. I was very much on the alert, sizing up every stranger I encountered. I happened to notice a gentleman who looked a little rough around the edges, probably from the long ride. While thinking that he looked a little suspicious to me, I chuckled to myself, because I remembered an episode in *The Lucy Show* in which Lucy was on a train ride and thought she spotted a suspicious person. She caused all kinds of problems when she thought the innocent gentleman was a train robber.

As I was watching the man on my train and his stern countenance, several people started gathering around him with much interest. Being a curious young man, I decided to slowly move closer to the gathering to see if I could hear what they were talking about. I was startled to find that they were talking about the second coming of Christ! They were discussing the signs of the times and how things were lining up for Christ's imminent return. I enthusiastically joined the discussion, spilling out loads of questions. As we finally pulled into Mexico City, I thanked this gentleman and introduced myself. He shook my hand and told me his name was Hal Lindsey. He later wrote the best seller *The Late Great Planet Earth*. Since that wonderful encounter, I have been studying Bible prophecy. And following Hal's recommendation, I attended Dallas Theological Seminary. I became intrigued by how explicitly God orchestrated His plans for mankind and His itinerary for the ages.

One warm Sunday afternoon while I was still a seminary student, I decided to go for a pizza lunch after church with some of my friends. We entered a place called Shakey's Pizza. Little did I know that that lunch would set me up for a long and exciting journey of biblical discovery. The restaurant was designed so that everyone sat together, strangers and all, on benches at long tables. A nice baldheaded gentleman sat right across from me. I noticed an odd phenomenon about this man. It appeared that smoke was coming up from the back of his head. When I gently brought that to his attention, he turned as red as a beet and sheepishly brought out from behind his back a cigarette. He informed me that he was Jewish and had recently accepted Jesus as his Savior and Messiah. When he had seen our group of churchgoers come in, he had immediately tried to hide his cigarette, because he didn't know what Christians thought about smoking. We had a good laugh about it, and then we talked about the many evidences that convinced him that Jesus is the Messiah. Also to my delight, we talked about Christ's impending return. He was so much fun to talk with because he was very knowledgeable and humorous. This wonderful Jewish man turned out to be Zola Levitt. Later, he became a prolific writer and teacher. He told me something that stuck with me for years. He said that many of the secrets of God's plan for the ages were in the Levitical feasts. I kept thinking about that statement off and on for a long time before I finally acted on it. Ever since then, I have had a nagging curiosity about the feasts. So recently I decided to research all that I could about them.

I thought it would be a good idea to seek insight from Jewish rabbis. I made inquiry of both messianic and orthodox rabbis. They all gave me a similar observation: "If you seriously study the feasts, you will experience a blessing that will be beyond your expectation." I appreciated the encouragement, and later I found out they knew what they were talking about. They meant what they said. I have been blessed beyond my wildest dreams. I have been totally stunned at how much information God has packed into the observances of the seven feasts in Leviticus 23.

God opened several opportunities for me to teach what I had discovered about His seven feasts. God emphatically said in Leviticus 23:2 that these were His feasts that He designed for the Jews to observe and learn about Him. I noticed that the teaching about the feasts had the same effect on the people that I taught as it did me. They were greatly blessed by what God revealed about Himself in the observance of the feasts. I found that the information encourages, comforts, motivates, and strengthens one's faith.

One evening I was having dinner at a café in a hotel. To my delight I realized that Tim LaHaye, coauthor of the *Left Behind* series, was sitting at the next table. I took the opportunity to strike up a conversation with him and ask him some questions about prophecy. The conversation got around to the feasts. When I shared with him some of the things I had discovered from my visits with the rabbis and other sources, he was just as surprised at the information as I had been. He then encouraged me to write a book about my findings. As a result of his persuasion and encouragement, I decided to write this book, taking each feast one at a time and explaining them in terms of how I have discovered the mysteries unfold.

As you study the feasts with me, I hope this will be a life-changing adventure for you, just as it has been for me.

INTRODUCTION

God revealed His plan for the ages by the details of the feasts, both biblical and traditional. When you attend a concert or a play, you receive a printed program that tells you what and when each act will be performed. These seven feasts of God are His program laid out for us to know what Christ, His Son, is doing in the world. In studying the feasts, it became obvious to me that they fall into two different groups: the spring feasts and the fall feasts. These separate groupings are significant, and the timing between the feasts is important. The spring feasts picture the events surrounding Jesus Christ's first coming, and the fall feasts picture the events surrounding His second coming. To illustrate this point, I have placed a photo of a lamb at the beginning of each chapter that discusses one of the spring feasts, because Christ came first as the Lamb of

God. Likewise, at the beginning of each chapter that discusses one of the fall feasts, I have placed a photo of a lion, because Christ will come in His second coming as the Lion of Judah.

An important thing I noticed was that God said these feasts are His feasts and not Israel's. Leviticus 23:1–2 reads: "The Lord spoke again to Moses, saying, 'Speak to the sons of Israel, and say to them, "The Lord's appointed times which you shall proclaim as holy convocations—My appointed times are these."'" God emphasized that these appointed times are His appointed times.

If we are to understand the times, we must become familiar with the Hebrew calendar. In our modern-day American culture, we are accustomed to the Gregorian calendar. This calendar is based on the sun, while the Hebrew calendar is based on the moon. This is why the dates of the feasts continue to float or appear at different days each year on our calendar. In addition, just as today there is both a secular and fiscal year calendar, the Jews have both a secular and a sacred calendar. The Jewish sacred calendar is synonymous with a fiscal year calendar because it is based on their harvest seasons. This is why God said in Exodus12:2, "This month shall be the beginning of the months for you . . ." referring to the month of Nisan. In contrast, the secular calendar begins with month of Tishri.

The first two spring feasts are Passover (*Pesach*) and Unleavened Bread (*Hag Ha Matzah*). One follows immediately after the other because the Feast of Unleavened Bread is an extension of the Passover Feast. Leviticus 23:4–8 explains them in this way: "These are the appointed times of the Lord, holy convocations which you shall proclaim at the times appointed for them. In the first month, on the fourteenth day of the month at twilight is the Lord's Passover. Then on the fifteenth day of the same month there is the Feast of Unleavened Bread to the Lord; for seven days you shall eat unleavened bread. On the first day you shall have a holy convocation; you shall not do any laborious work. But for seven days you shall present an offering by fire to the Lord. On the seventh day is a holy convocation; you shall not do any laborious work."

The "month" refers to the month of Abib, which was changed to Nisan after the Babylonian captivity. On our calendar it falls in March or April. Moses spoke to the people in Exodus 13:3–4: "Moses said to the people, 'Remember this day in which you went out from Egypt, from the house of slavery; for by a powerful hand the Lord brought you out from this place. And nothing leavened shall be eaten. On this day in the month of Abib, you are about to go forth.'"

Then we come to the Feast of Firstfruits (*Yom Bikkurim*) in Leviticus 23:9–11: "Then the Lord spoke to Moses, saying, 'Speak to the sons of Israel, and say to them, "When you enter the land which I am going to give to you and reap its harvest, then you shall bring in the sheaf of the firstfruits of your harvest to the priest. He shall wave the sheaf before the Lord for you to be accepted; on the day after the Sabbath the priest shall wave it."'"

The last of the spring feasts is the Feast of Pentecost. Since it takes place fifty days after Firstfruits, it falls in May or June. The Hebrew name for the feast is *Shavuot*. In the Old

Testament, this feast is called the Feast of Weeks, commemorating the giving of the Torah to Israel. Leviticus 23:15–16 says: "You shall also count for yourselves from the day after the Sabbath, from the day when you brought in the sheaf of the wave offering; there shall be seven complete Sabbaths. You shall count fifty days to the day after the seventh Sabbath; then you shall present a new grain offering to the Lord."

All four spring feasts have been fulfilled, as I will discuss later. There are three more feasts that have yet to be fulfilled, and these are called the fall feasts. They are known as the Feast of Trumpets, the Day of Atonement, and the Feast of Tabernacles. These feasts fall in September or October on our Gregorian calendar.

The Feast of Trumpets (Rosh Hashanah, the Jewish New Year) starts on the first day of Tishri, which is the seventh month of the sacred calendar but the first day of the secular calendar. Leviticus 23:23–25 says: "Again the Lord spoke to Moses, saying, 'Speak to the sons of Israel, saying, "In the seventh month on the first of the month you shall have a rest, a reminder by blowing of *trumpets*, a holy convocation. You shall not do any laborious work, but you shall present an offering by fire to the Lord."'" The significance of this feast is quite startling. In a later chapter, I will discuss this very exciting feast. It might change your thinking about some things.

The Day of Atonement (*Yom Kippur*) is the tenth day of Tishri. It is a very solemn day for the Jews because it is judgment day. We read in Leviticus 23:26–32: "The Lord spoke to Moses, saying, 'On exactly the tenth day of this seventh month is the Day of Atonement; it shall be a holy convocation for you, and you shall humble your souls and present an offering by fire to the Lord. You shall not do any work on this same day, for it is a day of atonement, to make atonement on your behalf before the Lord your God. If there is any person who will not humble himself on this same day, he shall be cut off from his people. As for any person who does any work on this same day, that person I will destroy from among his people. You shall do no work at all. It is to be a perpetual statute throughout your generations in all your dwelling places. It is to be a Sabbath of complete rest to you, and you shall humble your souls; on the ninth of the month at evening, from evening until evening you shall keep your Sabbath.'"

Finally, we come to the last of the fall feasts, the Feast of Tabernacles, or Booths (*Sukkot*). This feast is to be observed on the fifteenth day of Tishri. This last feast is very festive because it occurs after the harvests have been completed, and God's gracious provisions are to be enjoyed with great celebration. Leviticus 23:33–36 reads: "Again the Lord spoke to Moses, saying: 'Speak to the sons of Israel, saying, "On the fifteenth of this seventh month is the Feast of Booths for seven days to the Lord. On the first day is a holy convocation; you shall do no laborious work of any kind. For seven days you shall present an offering by fire to the Lord. On the eighth day you shall have a holy convocation and present an offering by fire to the Lord; it is an assembly. You shall do no laborious work."'"

You might notice that an eighth day follows the seven-day celebration, which seems somewhat strange. It turns out that

→ xix ←

this eighth day is very exciting in its significance to God's total plan of the ages. I will examine that also in a later chapter.

The feasts make it apparent that God wants us to understand His plans through all five of our senses. Keep in mind, the feasts may fall on any day of the week and are considered a high sabbath in contrast to a weekly sabbath. Also remember that the four spring feasts have been fulfilled in the events relating to Christ's first coming. We are looking forward to the fulfillment of the remaining fall feasts relating to Christ's second coming.

The Hebrew Calendar

HEBREW (lunar-solar)		LENGTH	GREGORIAN
1	Nisan	30 days	March-April
2	Iyar	29 days	April-May
3	Sivan	30 days	May-June
4	Tammuz	29 days	June-July
5	Av	30 days	July-August
6	Elul	29 days	August-September
7	Tishri	30 days	September-October
8	Cheshvan	29 or 30 days	October-November
9	Kislev	30 or 29 days	November-December
10	Tevet	29 days	December-January
11	Shevat	30 days	January-February
12	Adar I (leap years only)	30 days	February-March
13	Adar (called Adar II in leap years)	29 days	February-March

One

THE PASSOVER

The First of the Spring Feasts

The First Passover

Many Christians are familiar with the events of the first Passover, but we are confronted with some very intriguing facts when we study the particulars. When we read that God caused ten plagues to torment the Egyptians after the Pharaoh stubbornly refused to let the Jews leave Egypt, we are tempted to just absorb the story and move on to the next event. But God was doing much more to the Egyptians than just pressuring Pharaoh to release the Jews. He was teaching them about their many false gods and administering harsh judgment for their idolatry. As an example, when God turned the Nile to blood, He was attacking their worship of Khnum, their god of the river. Likewise, the plague of frogs that followed was an attack on Heqt, the frog-headed goddess of resurrection. She was the wife of Khnum. The other plagues also were attacks relating to other gods. Lice stopped the Egyptians' sacrifices because of cleanness issues, and swarms of flies were a sign against Beelzebub, prince of the air, because flies were always flying around his ears. Livestock suffered disease for punishment against Apis, the sacred bull, while boils were opposed to Imhotep, the god of medical cures. Hailstones showed the weakness of Nut, the sky goddess; locusts opposed Nepri, the grain god; darkness was an attack against Re, the sun god; and the death of the firstborn attacked all of the gods.

We read in Exodus 12:2–3: "This month shall be the beginning of months for you; it is to be the first month of the year to you. 'Speak to all the congregation of Israel, saying, "On the tenth of this month, they are each one to take a lamb for themselves, according to their fathers' households, a lamb for each household."'" The lamb was an attack on the Egyptian god Amon, the head of all their gods. He was presented in human form, but his animal was a ram. The month of the Passover was also in the month of Nisan, the month when the Egyptians celebrated the deity of Amon.

I wondered if there was also any significance to taking a lamb on the tenth day of the month for the household. I became more curious when I read further in the Exodus passage. It states in Exodus 12:6: "You shall keep it until the fourteenth day of the same month, then the whole assembly of the congregation of Israel is to kill it at twilight." Why the fourteenth day? I discovered two very interesting answers. One, each day that the lamb was in captivity was to remind them of one hundred years of captivity in Egypt for a total of four hundred years. Two, for four days the lamb would become a pet to the family, so when it was sacrificed, they would know the gravity of the penalty of their sins. It is also important to note that the fourteenth was the full moon, which the Egyptians considered the pinnacle of Amon's power. Sacrificing the lamb demonstrated that Amon had no power at all.

We read further in Exodus 12:7: "Moreover, they shall take some of the blood and put it on the two doorposts and on the lintel of the houses in which they eat it." Many of us have heard that if you were to connect the smears of blood on the doorway, it would form a cross. It is a legitimate observation, but it would seem if a smear of blood were also on the threshold, this would represent a more complete picture of the cross. However, when I stumbled upon Hebrews 10:29, it became clear to me why the blood of the lamb was not to be placed on the threshold. The author of Hebrews states, "How much severer punishment do you think he will deserve who has trampled under foot the Son of God, and has regarded as unclean the blood of the covenant by which he was sanctified, and has insulted the Spirit of grace." While pondering this image, I surmised that there might be many more pictures that God had provided for us.

I visited with David Schiller, a teacher of the Torah at a messianic congregation, Eitz Chaim, in Richardson, Texas. He shared with me many fascinating things about the Passover lamb. He explained that there is historical evidence that the lamb was roasted upright on a pomegranate pole with a crossbar through its shoulders. This obviously would bring to mind the cross. The pomegranate pole was used, because as a dry wood it would not boil. Boiling was prohibited in preparing the lamb. Schiller mentioned another observation from tradition: the pomegranate is symbolic of royalty and the priesthood. Another notable point is that the entrails were tied around the head so everything could be roasted evenly without boiling. This resembles the crown of thorns. Other sources verified Schiller's descriptions. One very captivating article on this subject is "The Crucifixion of the Paschal Lamb," written by Joseph Tabory for *Jewish Quarterly Review* (see Bibliography for more information). Another good explanation of the parallels can be found in Alfred Edersheim's book *The Temple: Its Ministry and Services* (see chapter 12, "The Paschal Feast and the Lord's Supper").

We must remember that the feasts not only provide historical teachings and spiritual implications but also prophetic applications. When each Jewish family was choosing their lamb on the tenth day of Nisan for Passover, God was revealing His Lamb at the triumphant entry of Jesus, the fulfillment of Zechariah 9:9. Dr. Harold Hoehner, a professor of mine when I was at Dallas Theological Seminary, did extensive work on the dates and chronology of the life of Jesus Christ. Based on the most accurate historical evidences, he came to the conclusion that Jesus' triumphant entry was on the tenth day of Nisan, or March 30 AD 33. He wrote of his discoveries and analysis in the article "Daniel's Seventy Weeks and New Testament Chronology," which appeared on page 135 of the January–March 1975 edition of *Bibliotheca Sacra* (see Bibliography).

Along with these observations, we must take note that on the fourteenth day, at the same hour the lamb was being sacrificed at the Temple, Jesus, the Lamb of God, was also being crucified on the cross. This is why the historical observation of the lamb sacrificed upright on a pole, as Christ was sacrificed upright on a cross, paints such a meaningful picture.

The Lamb

Let's take a closer look at the lamb. A number of years ago I heard Jimmy DeYoung, an outstanding news commentator and Bible teacher, make a presentation at a Bible prophecy conference. Since it was during the Christmas season, he was teaching about the birth of Jesus in the first chapter of Luke. He read to us Luke 2:8–12: "In the same region there were some shepherds staying out in the fields and keeping watch over their flock by night. And an angel of the Lord suddenly stood before them, and the glory of the Lord shone around them; and they were terribly frightened. And the angel said to them, 'Do not be afraid; for behold, I bring you good news of a great joy which shall be for all the people; for today in the city of David there has been born for you a Savior, who is Christ the Lord. This will be a sign for you: you will find a baby wrapped in cloths, and lying in a manger.'"

Dr. DeYoung then asked the audience a surprising question: "Did you ever wonder why this was a sign?" This left us all speechless. I had to admit to myself that I had never even questioned it. Why was it a sign? Dr. DeYoung had us turn to the book of Micah. We were all familiar with Micah 5:2, which prophesied that the Messiah would be born in Bethlehem, but many of us were not familiar with Micah 4:8, which prophesied that He would be announced at the tower of the flock (*Migdal Eder*). Dr. DeYoung, who had lived in Jerusalem for a number of years, told us that Migdal Eder was a two-story tower that had been built in a pasture outside Bethlehem. The remains of the tower had recently been discovered.

Dr. DeYoung explained that the shepherds in the field had not all been the lowly shepherds that we had always assumed. They were actually priests from the temple who were doing shepherding work to assist in the birthing of the sacrificial lambs so that they would be unblemished for sacrifice. While the shepherds were keeping watch over the flock from the top floor of the tower, the shepherd-priests would bring the pregnant sheep in from the field to the tower's bottom floor, where the sheep would give birth. As soon as a lamb was born, the priests would wrap it with strips of cloths made from old priestly undergarments. This was done to keep the lamb from getting blemished. The priests would then place the lamb onto a manger to make sure it would not get trampled. Wow! So when these shepherd-priests went into Bethlehem and saw the baby Jesus wrapped in cloths, lying in a manger, they must have exclaimed, "There is the Lamb of God, prepared for sacrifice, unblemished!" They had to be excited beyond description, because they were the only ones who could have understood the sign. It was just for them from God. It was personal!

I presume that Jesus' swaddling cloths were from the same source as the lambs' cloths. Mary's cousin, Elizabeth, was married to the priest Zacharias. Elizabeth could have given her the cloths made from the priestly undergarments. It is highly probable that the first clothes that Jesus wore were the clothes of a priest. What a sign! I was so intrigued by this that I did some further research. These historical observations and parallels were confirmed by many messianic rabbis and the renowned historical writer Alfred Edersheim. I also sought out help from Bob Ibach, an experienced archaeologist, who had done some digs in Israel. He found the written account and pictures of the discovery of "the tower of the flock," Migdal Eder. This whole insight made the account of the announcement of Jesus' birth astounding and even more exciting!

More and more facts began to unfold in my research. I was talking further with David Schiller, my Jewish teacher and friend, about what I had learned about the shepherds and the lambs. He amazed me with some more historical insights. He explained that each Jewish family would put the family name around the neck of their lamb that they took to the Temple to be sacrificed. They did this to make sure they received their own lamb back for the Passover dinner. I wondered if there was any significance to this piece of trivia. As I was contemplating this, Schiller pointed out to me a particular object found in most of the paintings of Christ on the cross. There was a small sign at the top of the cross that looked like four letters: "INRI." I discovered that this was an abbreviation of the sign that Pontius Pilot placed on the cross as seen in John 19:19: "Pilate also wrote an inscription, and put it on the cross. It was written, 'JESUS THE NAZARENE, THE KING OF THE JEWS.'" I learned that the letters were the first letters of each of the nouns in the inscription in Latin. I contacted my daughter Ruth, who is very good with Latin, and asked her to show me the inscription in the Latin Vulgate. That confirmed it: *"Iesus Nazarenus Rex Iudaeorum" (INRI)*.

Then Schiller opened my eyes to an incredible observation. Since the inscription had been in three languages—Latin, Greek, and Hebrew—he transliterated it for me from Hebrew to English. I saw before me these words: *"Y'Shua HaNatzri V'Melech HaYehudim."* I was absolutely stunned when I took the first letters of each of these words. It spelled "YHVH," the Tetragrammaton form of the name of God! YHVH and YHWH can be used interchangeably. When this technique of abbreviating is used, the title on the cross in the actual Hebraic script undeniably reveals the name of God. In English, the name is pronounced "Yahweh!" Just like the Jews put their family name on their lamb for sacrifice at the Temple, God put His name on His Lamb for His family, which includes you and me! God gave us so many pictures in order that we could understand the magnitude of His loving grace!

The Passover Dinner

Now we look at the Passover dinner. Exodus 12:8 says: "They shall eat the flesh that same night, roasted with fire, and they

shall eat it with unleavened bread and bitter herbs." I learned that
the Passover dinners varied slightly from household to household and from different generations, but the main picture and
the order of the feast were the same. I consulted the messianic
Hagaddah, which gives the order of the Seder and the meaning
of each tradition of the feast. Some aspects of the feast captured
my curiosity. The most interesting was the four different cups
of wine and their meaning as a part of the Jewish tradition.
The four cups were to remind everyone of the four promises in
Exodus 6:6–7: "Say, therefore, to the sons of Israel, 'I am the
Lord, and I will bring you out from under the burdens of the
Egyptians, and I will deliver you from their bondage. I will also
redeem you with an outstretched arm and with great judgments.
Then I will take you for My people, and I will be your God; and
you shall know that I am the Lord your God, who brought you
out from under the burdens of the Egyptians.'"

I discovered that each cup had its own name in order to
designate its significance in the remembrance of the respective
key phrases in the aforementioned promises from Exodus. I
also became aware that the names of the cups varied somewhat among different rabbis. I will refer to the names that seem
most commonly used. The promise that each cup signifies
is the most important aspect. The first cup that is taken at
the beginning of the observance is often called the "Cup of
Blessing or Sanctification." It refers to the phrase "I will bring
you out." God promises to separate them from Egypt, which
also pictures sanctification in being separated from our sin.
Just before the meal the second cup is taken, which is called

by some the "Cup of Praise," giving praise to God for His promise, "I will deliver you from bondage." After the meal all participants partake of the third cup, which is called "Cup of Redemption." At the Last Supper, Jesus referred to this third cup in Matthew 26:28: "For this is My blood of the covenant, which is poured out for many for forgiveness of sins." This is the cup that we as Christians partake of at communion. We have been partaking of the third cup!

The fourth cup taken at the end of the observance is commonly called the "Cup of the Kingdom." I noticed that Jesus made a change in the Seder, which He observed as the Last Supper. He apparently refrained from drinking from the fourth cup. We read in Matthew 26:29: "But I say to you, I will not drink of this fruit of the vine from now on until that day when I drink it new with you in My Father's kingdom."

It became obvious that Jesus did not want to drink of the fourth cup because everything He did was to fulfill prophecy. Since the kingdom was not yet to be established, He skipped that cup, sang a hymn, and left. I discussed this in correspondence with messianic rabbi Michael Short of Phoenix, Arizona. He confirmed that this observation was accurate, but he said there was another reason that Jesus did not drink of the fourth cup. Hearing what that reason was absolutely astounded me! Rabbi Short revealed that it had to do with the Jewish wedding tradition. When a Jewish lad would propose marriage to a prospective bride, he would offer her a cup of wine. If she drank it, she was accepting the betrothal. He would then inform her that he was to go to his father's house to prepare a place for her. She would typically respond, "When are you coming back?" The prospective groom would reply by saying, "Only my father knows!"

Have you heard this dialogue before? Jesus and His disciples had this very same discussion the night of the Last Supper. After the disciples drank of the third cup, which was symbolically the "Cup of Betrothal," Jesus told them that He was going to His Father's house to prepare a place for them. He said, "I go to prepare a place for you. If I go and prepare a place for you, I will come again, and receive you to Myself; that where I am, there you may be also" (John 14:2–3). Jesus was obviously talking to His future bride, the Church. When the place or chamber that the bridegroom spent time preparing was complete, his father would tell him that it was time for him to retrieve his bride. The bride and groom would then celebrate their togetherness at the father's house for seven days. After the seven days, the bride and groom would come out of the chamber to observe a wedding feast in their honor. The bride and groom would start the feast by drinking together a cup of wine that was called the "Cup of Consummation." This cup, according to Rabbi Short, is the same as the fourth cup of the Seder's "Cup of the Kingdom"!

When Christians take the Cup of Redemption in the communion service, we are actually accepting our betrothal to the Lord. Eventually, in the Kingdom, we will drink the "Cup of Consummation" with our Lord at the Marriage Feast of the Lamb. That will be the fourth cup, the Kingdom Cup of the Last Supper. In reality, the Last Supper was unfinished. So after a long break, it will resume again with all believers present in the kingdom to complete it. If Leonardo da Vinci wants to repaint the Last Supper in its completed form, he will have to come up with a mighty big canvas.

Now let us look at the bread that is referred to in the Seder. It is called *matzah*. If you purchase matzah bread at a store, it looks a lot like a large saltine cracker. It actually is bread that has no leaven in it, which gives it the flat, cracker-like appearance. The matzah bread is baked in such a way that it is pierced with tiny holes in rows, resulting in a striped appearance with brown spots resembling bruises. Today, since the temple is no longer in existence for sacrificing the lamb, the rabbis have ruled that the matzah bread could suffice for the lamb. This fact ties in beautifully with Isaiah 53:5: "But he was *pierced* for our transgressions, he was *bruised* for our iniquities; the chastisement for our peace *was* upon Him; and by His *stripes* we are healed" (NKJV; emphasis mine).

During the Seder, a three-compartment pouch called *matzah tosh* is placed at the head of the table. Each compartment has a piece of matzah in it. Jews understand that the three compartments refer to Abraham, Isaac, and Jacob. Christians recognize that the compartments can also refer to the Father, Son, and Holy Spirit. The parallels are evident: Abraham-God, Isaac-Jesus, and Jacob-the Holy Spirit. Let me explain. God chose Abraham out of the Chaldees just as God the Father, according to Ephesians 1:4–5, chose us before the foundation of the world. Likewise, Isaac, on Mount Moriah, typified substitutionary atonement, the atonement that Jesus the Son provided when He shed His blood for us. Sanctification is illustrated by Jacob's life as he grew in his relationship with God; likewise, the Holy Spirit helps believers mature in their walk with the Lord. It is traditional that the matzah in the middle compartment is removed and broken in half. The half piece is called the *afikomen* and is wrapped in a cloth and hidden for later retrieval by the children at the end of the meal. When a child finds the afikomen, he is given a gift, usually money. I understand the gift today a child commonly receives is five dollars. What's fascinating is that five in the Hebraic number system stands for God's grace! To me, this tradition illustrates believers receiving spiritual gifts when they find Christ as explained in Ephesians 4:7: "But to each one of us grace was given according to the measure of Christ's gift."

The Greek meaning of afikomen is "that which is coming." It can simply refer to dessert, but many take it to mean "he who is coming." According to Jewish tradition, Messiah will come at Passover to bring redemption. This is why a place is left at the table for Elijah, the forerunner of Messiah (Malachi 4:5).

Two

THE FEAST OF UNLEAVENED BREAD

The Second of the Spring Feasts

The Feast of Unleavened Bread is an extension of the Passover. "Then on the fifteenth day of the same month there is the Feast of Unleavened Bread to the Lord; for seven days you shall eat unleavened bread" (Lev. 23:6). Additionally, we read in Exodus 12:17–20: "You shall also observe the Feast of Unleavened Bread, for on this very day I brought your hosts out of the land of Egypt; therefore you shall observe this day throughout your generations as a permanent ordinance. In the first month, on the fourteenth day of the month at evening, you shall eat unleavened bread, until the twenty-first day of the month at evening. Seven days there shall be no leaven found in your houses; for whoever eats what is leavened, that person shall be cut off from the congregation of Israel, whether he is an alien or a native of the land. You shall not eat anything leavened; in all your dwellings you shall eat unleavened bread."

Starting with Passover and continuing through the next seven days, the Jews are not to eat any leavened bread of any kind. They cannot even have any leavened bread anywhere in their homes or places of business. I have a friend who is a professional photographer. He received a contract to go to Israel to take pictures of various breads at a bakery for an advertisement. We wondered what the bread store would do during the Feast of Unleavened Bread. We had a good chuckle when we found out the answer. The bakery would sell the place to a Gentile for seven days and then buy it back.

Bedikat Chametz

There is a curious custom that many Jewish families participate in to prepare for the week of Passover and Feast of Unleavened Bread. It is called *Bedikat Chametz*. This custom is a kind of game to teach the children about how the Lord cleanses us of our sin in our daily walk with Him. The game consists of candles, a wooden spoon, a feather, ten leavened crumbs of bread, and a furnace of fire. The father of the household gives each child a candle, and the children go through their home looking for the ten leavened crumbs that have been placed in various locations around the house by the mother. When the children see a crumb, they call out, "Father, Father, we have found leaven!" He comes and gently brushes the crumb onto the wooden spoon with the feather and carries the crumb to a furnace to be burned. This illustrates that if we walk in the light of God's Word, that light reveals our sin to us. When we call out to our heavenly Father, He gently takes away our sin. The wooden spoon is symbolic of the wooden cross of Christ. This game teaches the children about sanctification. We read in 1 Corinthians 5:7–8: "Clean out the old leaven so that you may be a new lump, just as you are in fact unleavened. For Christ our Passover also has been sacrificed. Therefore let us celebrate the feast, not with old leaven, nor with the leaven of malice and wickedness, but with the unleavened bread of sincerity and truth."

The Feast of Unleavened Bread teaches the concept of being in fellowship with the Lord. The Lord has always sought to have fellowship with us rather than the other way around. It all became quite evident from the very beginning with Adam in the Garden of Eden. We read in Genesis 3:8–9 about the events that took place right after the first couple sinned: "They heard the sound of the Lord God walking in the garden in the cool of the day, and the man and his wife hid themselves from the presence of the Lord God among the trees of the garden. Then the Lord God called to the man, and said to him, 'Where are you?'" We see that God was the one who was seeking the fellowship. Later in history, we learn that the Lord was still seeking the fellowship of mankind when He was encouraging the Jews to hurry up and finish the building of the temple. The first thing God said through the prophet Zechariah was: "Return to Me . . . that I may return to you"

(Zech. 1:3). He was saying in effect, "Hurry up, for I am moving into the neighborhood to have fellowship with you!"

Fellowship with God had been broken starting with the first couple. We all are familiar with Genesis 2:15–17: "Then the Lord God took the man and put him into the Garden of Eden to cultivate it and keep it. The Lord God commanded the man, saying, 'From any tree of the garden you may eat freely; but from the tree of the knowledge of good and evil you shall not eat, for in the day that you eat from it you will surely die.'" It is important that we pay close attention to the expressions "eat freely" and "surely die." According to C.F. Keil and F. Delitzsch in *Biblical Commentary on the Old Testament*, (Vol.1, p. 85 – see Bibliography), this sentence structure is difficult to translate in the Hebrew language. When an infinitive absolute precedes a finite verb, the verb is intensified. Technically, the literal translation of the phrase "surely die" is "to die you die," or "die in your dying." In Genesis 3:2–4, we read: "The woman said to the serpent, 'From the fruit of the trees of the garden we may *eat*; but from the fruit of the tree which is in the middle of the garden, God has said, "You shall not eat from it or *touch it*, or you will *die*'" (emphasis mine). Eve, while trying to recite God's command to the serpent, dropped the infinitive absolutes. By doing that, she verbally minimized the magnitude of God's grace and justice. She did even more: she added to the command, *"or touch it."* This is exactly what people still do today! They try to add legalism to God's grace, weakening the concept of His righteousness. Interestingly enough, when the serpent responded, he replaced the infinitive absolute even in his deceptive statement: "You *surely will not die!*" The serpent knew God's command better than Eve did!

Believers are to live a sin-free life to maintain fellowship with God. This is done through the continual cleansing available to us by Christ's blood as stated in 1 John 1:7–8, "But if we walk in the light as He Himself is in the light, we have fellowship with one another, and the blood of Jesus His Son cleanses us from all sin. If we say we have no sin, we are deceiving ourselves, and the truth is not in us."

Fellowship and Sanctification

In what we call the Upper Room Discourse, Jesus taught Peter the meaning of having continual fellowship with God. We read in John 13:10: "Jesus said to him, 'He who has bathed needs only to wash his feet, but is completely clean; and you are clean, but not all of you.'" In 1 John 1:7–8, the apostle John provides further explanation of Jesus' teachings on continual fellowship. Sin itself cannot break our fellowship with God, since Christ's blood continually cleanses us from all sin. However, the denial, rationalization, or ignoring of sin revealed to us by the Holy Spirit causes us to lose our fellowship with God. If we fall out of fellowship because we deny our sin and we later confess that sin, God restores our fellowship with Him as we see in 1 John 1:9: "If we confess our sins, He is faithful and righteous to forgive us our sins and to cleanse us from all unrighteousness." 1 John 1:7 describes the maintenance of our fellowship, and 1 John 1:9 the restoration of our fellowship.

Speaking of sanctification, several years ago I had the opportunity to visit Dr. S. Lewis Johnson, former professor of New Testament and Systematic Theology at Dallas Seminary, before he passed away. While we were enjoying a good cup of coffee, he shared with me a clear-cut way to present the four phases of sanctification. I quickly took notes, because I liked his simple explanation. The Bible teaches us of four phases in the process of sanctification: preparatory, positional, progressive, and prospective.

Preparatory sanctification is the process the Holy Spirit uses to bring us to the point of salvation. He worked with us long before we knew Him. 2 Thessalonians 2:13 says: "God has chosen you from the beginning for salvation through sanctification by the Spirit and faith in the truth." Likewise 1 Peter 1:1–2 speaks of those "who are chosen, according to the foreknowledge of God the Father, by the sanctifying work of the Spirit."

Positional sanctification refers to our salvation, the moment we put our faith in Jesus. This is also referred to as justification, when we are declared righteous. Paul, speaking to new believers in I Corinthians 6:11, reminds them that they are washed, sanctified, and justified in the Lord Jesus Christ. Also, we read in Hebrews 10:10: "By His will we have been sanctified through the offering of the body of Jesus Christ once for all."

Progressive sanctification describes the spiritual growth of the believer as he becomes more Christ-like in his walk. This phase is usually what we think of when we refer to sanctification. It is also the phase of sanctification pictured by the Feast of Unleavened Bread. 2 Corinthians 7:1 says: "Therefore, having these promises, beloved, let us cleanse ourselves from all defilement of flesh and spirit, perfecting holiness in the fear of God." Also 2 Corinthians 3:18 explains: "But we all, with unveiled face, beholding as in a mirror the glory of the Lord, are being transformed into the same image from glory to glory, just as from the Lord, the Spirit."

Prospective or ultimate sanctification is what Christians are looking forward to. It is when we receive our new bodies without the sin nature, and truly live without sin. This phase is called glorification. We read about it in Romans 8:29: "For those whom He foreknew, He also predestined to become conformed to the image of His Son, that He would be the firstborn among many brethren." And in 1 Thessalonians 5:23–24, we read: "Now may the God of peace Himself sanctify you entirely; and may your spirit and soul and body be preserved complete, without blame at the coming of our Lord Jesus Christ. Faithful is He who calls you, and He also will bring it to pass."

I came across the following admonition to Gentile believers at a messianic congregation: "Let your Jewish friends know the matzah of Passover is central to your faith as well, because of the Jewish Messiah, 'the Lamb of God who takes away the sin of the world'" (John 1:29).

Timing of Christ's Burial

As you can see, there are many pictures about the Messiah in these first two spring feasts. There are many more; we have merely scratched the surface. I believe, though, that the most important parallel of the feasts is the timing of their observance. While Jesus observed the Seder early, His death on the cross occurred at the time the lambs were being sacrificed at the temple. We read in Exodus 12:5–6: "Your lamb shall be an unblemished male a year old; you may take it from the sheep or from the goats. You shall keep it until the fourteenth day of the same month, then the whole assembly of the congregation of Israel is to kill it at twilight." *Twilight* is also translated in some texts as "between the evenings." According to Flavius Josephus (see *Josephus Complete Works*, refer to Bibliography), the Passover lambs were slain between 3:00–5:00 P.M. Thus, the sacrificing of the Paschal lambs at the temple corresponds to the time of Jesus' death at the ninth hour, 3:00 P.M. We read in Matthew 27:45–50: "Now from the sixth hour darkness fell upon all the land until the ninth hour. About the ninth hour Jesus cried out with a loud voice, saying, 'ELI, ELI, LAMA SABACHTHANI?' That is, 'MY GOD, MY GOD, WHY HAST THOU FORSAKEN ME?' And some of those who were standing there, when they heard it, began saying, 'This man is calling for Elijah.' Immediately one of them ran, and taking a sponge, he filled it with sour wine, and put it on a reed, and gave Him a drink. But the rest of them said, 'Let us see whether Elijah will come to save Him.'

And Jesus cried out again with a loud voice, and yielded up His spirit."

Jesus was buried on the first day of the Feast of Unleavened Bread. Two days before Jesus' crucifixion, He prepared His disciples by saying in Matthew 26:2: "You know that after two days the Passover is coming, and the Son of Man is to be delivered up for crucifixion." We read in John 19:31: "Then the Jews, because it was the day of preparation, so that the bodies should not remain on the cross on the Sabbath (for that Sabbath was a high day), asked Pilate that their legs might be broken, and that they might be taken away." Therefore, this Passover was not referring to a weekly Sabbath but a high Sabbath. According to the law in Deuteronomy 21:22–23, a body was not to remain exposed on a tree overnight, and certainly not on a Sabbath. Our sins were paid for on the cross on the fourteenth of Nisan, which was the Passover, and buried with Christ on the fifteenth of Nisan, which was the first day of the Feast of Unleavened Bread. The exact days of these feasts were the exact days that Jesus was crucified and buried. When things look like they are out of control, we must remember that God is still in control of all things. Paul reiterated this truth when he wrote, in 1 Corinthians 5:7: "For Christ our Passover also has been sacrificed."

Three

THE FEAST OF FIRSTFRUITS

The Third of the Spring Feasts

I was astounded that there were so many pictures and parallels in the first two feasts about Jesus Christ and His ministry. I expected that I would find some more surprises with the other two spring feasts: the Feast of Firstfruits and the Feast of Pentecost. I am happy to tell you that I was not at all disappointed. In fact, I was amazed at the information I discovered.

In Leviticus 23:9–11 we read: "Then the Lord spoke to Moses, saying, 'Speak to the sons of Israel, and say to them, "When you enter the land which I am going to give to you and reap its harvest, then you shall bring in the sheaf of the firstfruits of your harvest to the priest. He shall wave the sheaf before the Lord for you to be accepted; on the day after the Sabbath the priest shall wave it."'" I noticed two things right away. First, the Jews had to be in the Promised Land before they could observe this celebration that we call the Feast of Firstfruits. Second, they obviously could not observe it until the time of the harvest. This led me to study the harvest seasons of Israel. I had no idea that the facts of the harvests would open up a whole new line of discovery. As an experienced gardener, I am aware of the importance of the stages of the moon in planting and harvesting. I was impressed when I noticed that the planting and harvest cycles of Israel tie in closely with the positions of the moon.

Significance of the Moon to Crops

The four stages of the moon are important to raising crops: new moon, second quarter, full moon, and fourth quarter. When I studied forestry and soil science in college, I learned that the new moon gravitationally pulls water up through the soil and causes seeds to swell and burst. This makes it the best time to plant grain crops and other plants that are grown for above-ground produce. The increasing moonlight also causes a good balance between root development and leaf growth. The second quarter produces less gravitational pull, but provides vibrant moonlight. This is very beneficial to leaf growth. On the other hand, after the full moon, the moonlight is waning, but the gravitational pull is strong again. This combination makes it best for planting root crops. The fourth quarter provides less gravitational pull and moonlight. This is more of a resting period, which makes it an opportune time for cultivating and harvesting.

Harvest Phase

The harvesting times in Israel occur primarily during the fourth quarter of the moon. Since the feasts of God in Leviticus synchronize with the harvests, they also synchronize with the stages of the moon. The barley harvest is the first major harvest by the Jews. As it has been set up by God, the Feast of Firstfruits is tied to the harvest of the barley. For every harvest in Israel there are three phases: firstfruits, general harvest, and gleanings. The phase of firstfruits also has three phases of activity: marking, gathering, and presenting. The marking and gathering refers to the activity of identifying the first barley to mature and binding it in a sheaf, usually with a red cord to make it easy to spot. Then this chosen barley was brought to the priest to be presented by waving it before the Lord at the altar. As we read in Leviticus 23:10–11: "When you enter the land which I am going to give to you and reap its harvest, then you shall bring in the sheaf of the firstfruits of your harvest to the priest. He shall wave the sheaf before the Lord for you to be accepted; on the day after the Sabbath the priest shall wave it." This process or activity was done on the day after the weekly Sabbath, which fell during the week of the Feast of Unleavened Bread.

In 1 Corinthians 15:20–23, we read about Jesus Christ: "But now Christ has been raised from the dead, the firstfruits of those who are asleep. For since by a man came death, by a man also came the resurrection of the dead. For as in Adam all die, so also in Christ all will be made alive. But each in his own order: Christ the firstfruits, after that those who are Christ's at His coming." Also James 1:18 says: "In the exercise of His will He brought us forth by the word of truth, so that we would be a kind of firstfruits among His creatures." We know that Jesus rose from the dead on the day of the Feast of Firstfruits, because of Luke 24:1–3: "But on the first day of the week, at early dawn, they came to the tomb, bringing the spices which they had prepared. And they found the stone rolled away from the tomb, but when they entered, they did not find the body of the Lord Jesus." We should remember that the Feast of Firstfruits falls on the day after the weekly Sabbath. We are identified with Christ as our firstfruits, because of James 1:18.

The Harvests and the Resurrections

I have heard several Bible prophecy teachers allude to the various harvest times as pictures depicting the order of the resurrections of the saints. I decided to take a close look at the harvesting times and agricultural procedures that were used in Israel. I was astounded to discover that the order of harvests in Israel parallels the order of the resurrections of believers and the taking away of unbelievers. As we already observed, there is the barley harvest in the early spring. In a process called winnowing, the barley kernels are tossed into the wind to separate the kernels from the chaff. This is done because the head of the barley is very soft and easily winnowed. This reminds me of the birth of the church at Pentecost, when the Holy Spirit came like a wind and indwelt the believers as reported in Acts 2:1–2. There came a noise like a violent rushing wind that filled the room! In the order of the resurrections, the church is the first to be resurrected, just as the barley is the first to be harvested. It is like the church was winnowed from the world.

In the late spring, the wheat harvest begins. Since the head of the wheat is hard, it must be threshed or crushed to separate the wheat from the chaff. A man who is threshing the wheat stands on a large board with bits of glass or stones underneath it. This board is pulled by a horse over the wheat to do the crushing. I found it quite telling that the board is known as a *tribulum* in Latin. Many people, including Jews, will come to Christ in the Tribulation, as noted in Revelation 7:9–14. It is interesting that you can also tell the difference between a field of wheat and a field of barley. While the heads atop stalks of barley bend down like they are bowing in humility, the heads of the stalks of wheat stay straight up. I am reminded of Deuteronomy 31:27 where Moses said to the children of Israel: "For I know your rebellion, and your *stiff neck* (emphasis mine). If today, while I am yet alive with you, you have been rebellious against the Lord, then how much more after my death?" (NKJV) The church (the barley) will be resurrected first, while those who become believers (the wheat) in the Tribulation will be resurrected at the end of the Tribulation if they die in that period. In a sense they were harvested under the crushing of the *tribulum*.

At the beginning of the fall season, the fruit harvest is underway. The grapes are picked and then placed in the wine-presses. This is parallel to the judgment in Revelation 14:18–20: "'Put in your sharp sickle, and gather the clusters from the vine of the earth, because her grapes are ripe.' So the angel swung his sickle to the earth, and gathered the clusters from the vine of the earth, and threw them into the great wine press of the wrath of God. And the wine press was trodden outside the city, and blood came out from the wine press, up to the horses' bridles, for a distance of two hundred miles."

And finally, the gleanings are left in the fields. Leviticus 19:9–10 instructs the Jews *not to harvest the corners* of their fields and vineyards in order to leave grain and fruit for the poor. This is similar to Matthew 24:31, when the believers from the four winds of the earth will be gathered at the end of the Tribulation to enter the Kingdom. Since they did not die, they are *not resurrected*. Instead, they will move into the Kingdom to populate it for the next thousand years.

Let us summarize the harvest pictures. The first harvest is of barley in the spring that pictures the bride of Christ and her rapture before the Tribulation. The second harvest is of wheat at the end of spring and beginning of summer that pictures those who are saved in the Tribulation period and die. The Old Testament saints are also included with this group because they, like the tribulation saints, will be resurrected at the end of the Tribulation, as revealed in Daniel 12:1–2, Isaiah 26:19, and Revelation 20:4. The third harvest is of fruit in the fall that prefigures the unbelievers at the end of the Tribulation in the Battle of Armageddon who are taken away to wait for impending judgment at the Great White Throne at the end of the Millennium (Rev. 14:19). The rest of the unbelievers who are still alive at the end of the Tribulation will be taken away into eternal judgment immediately after the Sheep and Goat Judgment that Jesus explains in Matthew 25:41. They do not go through judgment twice. The last harvest is the gleanings that are not harvested and represents the tribulation saints who remain alive and enter the kingdom with their non-resurrected mortal bodies (Matt. 24:31).

We need to also look at remarkable parallels between the phases of the firstfruits and biblical prophecy. Remember that the phases of firstfruits are: *marking, gathering,* and *presenting.* The Church, identified as firstfruits in James 1:18, was sealed by the Holy Spirit according to Ephesians 1:13: "having also believed, you were sealed in Him with the Holy Spirit of promise." I consider this the *marking,* and the *gathering* will be the Rapture, while the *presenting* will occur at the Marriage Supper of the Lamb pictured in Revelation 19:7: "Let us rejoice and be glad and give the glory to Him, for the marriage of the Lamb has come and His bride has made herself ready."

We must also take note that the 144,000 Jewish evangelists in the Tribulation are likewise called the firstfruits in Revelation 14:4: "These have been purchased from among men as first fruits to God and to the Lamb." I would identify them as firstfruits of the wheat, since they are saved in the Tribulation. Their *marking* phase can be seen in Revelation 7:4 at their sealing: "And I heard the number of those who were sealed, one hundred and forty-four thousand sealed from every tribe of the sons of Israel." It is explained in the next verses that they are *gathered* from each of the twelve tribes. Of course, we can see their *presenting* phase in Revelation 14:3: "And they sang a new song before the throne and before the four living creatures and the elders; and no one could learn the song except the one hundred and forty-four thousand who had been purchased from the earth."

The Parallels with Christ

In his writings, D. Thomas Lancaster, an author of Jewish subjects and one of the main teachers in the ministries of First Fruits of Zion and also Vine of David, notes a parallel between the order of events of Christ's trial and the timing of the selection and gathering of the barley for firstfruits as stated in the Mishna (the collection of oral laws recorded in the Talmud). About the time that Caiaphas, the high priest, was trying Jesus, the servants of the disciples of the Sanhedrin were in the barley field judging the crop to decide which would be harvested for firstfruits. And on the day the Romans were binding up Jesus for crucifixion, the disciples of the Sanhedrin were binding up the barley sheaf for the firstfruits.

We read in John 20:1: "Now on the first day of the week Mary Magdalene came early to the tomb, while it was still dark, and saw the stone already taken away from the tomb." This was the day after the weekly Sabbath, being the day of the Feast of

Firstfruits. John 20:11–12 says: "But Mary was standing outside the tomb weeping; and so, as she wept, she stooped and looked into the tomb; and she saw two angels in white sitting, one at the head and one at the feet, where the body of Jesus had been lying." I couldn't help but notice something startling. Can you see it? Do you realize what Mary saw? She was actually seeing a live display of the mercy seat! That is very exciting. "She beheld two angels in white sitting, one at the head, and one at the feet, where the body of Jesus had been lying."

We immediately observe another thing in John 20:17, which had always puzzled me. When Mary recognized the resurrected Lord, He tells her, "Stop clinging to Me; for I have not yet ascended to the Father: but go to My brethren, and say to them, I ascend to my Father, and your Father; and my God, and your God." I never fully understood why He said that to Mary. Why couldn't she touch Him? I discovered the reason when I read what historian Flavius Josephus, a member of the Temple priesthood, wrote in *The Antiquities of the Jews* 3.10.5–6 (see *Josephus Complete Works*) about the barley. He explained that the Jews could not touch the barley before the Feast of Firstfruits. Once the barley sheaf was presented to God by the priest, the barley crop could be harvested for use. Since Jesus was the Firstfruits, He had to go to the Father before anyone could touch Him. We see that after He had been to the Father and back, Thomas could touch Him. As John 20:27 states: "Then He said to Thomas, 'Reach here with your finger, and see My hands; and reach here your hand, and put it into My side; and do not be unbelieving, but believing.'"

Until they harvested and offered the barley sheaf, or *omer*, in the temple, the rest of the crops were not deemed kosher (lawfully fit or acceptable). We read a great truth in 1 John 2:2: "And He is the propitiation for our sins: and not for ours only, but also for those of the whole world." We are now *kosher*, so to speak, because of what Christ has done on our behalf in fulfilling the Feast of Firstfruits to the very letter! The field of barley became kosher through the presentation of the firstfruits to God at the temple. The barley in the field did nothing to become kosher. In the same way, we have been made acceptable to God by Jesus, our Firstfruits, when He presented Himself to the Father. As the barley in the field did nothing to become kosher, likewise, we did nothing to become kosher except believe, of course.

We have observed in the events of history, it was by God's design that the activity of marking, gathering, and presenting the barley sheaf of Firstfruits coincided exactly with the death and resurrection of Christ. Why don't the Jews see the parallel? Many might be blinded now, but a day will come when they will see. This was promised in Zechariah 12:10: "I will pour out on the house of David and on the inhabitants of Jerusalem, the Spirit of grace and of supplication, so that they will look on Me whom they have pierced; and they will mourn for Him, as one mourns for an only son, and they will weep bitterly over Him, like the bitter weeping over a firstborn."

Four

THE FEAST OF PENTECOST

The Fourth of the Spring Feasts

Explicit parallels and contrasts are evident between the Feast of Pentecost in the New Testament and the Feast of Weeks in the Old Testament. The Feast of Weeks is the same feast the disciples observed in the New Testament, known as the Feast of Pentecost. At the first Feast of Weeks, God provided the law. God had given the children of Israel freedom from bondage and slavery, so He then gave them the law to guide them in living.

As slaves they were told what to do by their masters, but in freedom they needed guidance from their new Master, the Lord God of Heaven. It should be noted that God gave them freedom, salvation from slavery, before He gave them the law. Keeping the law was not a condition for receiving their freedom; it was a response to God's grace in setting them free. At the first Feast of Pentecost in the New Testament, God provided His Holy Spirit for guidance. The Feast of Weeks/Pentecost celebrates God's provisions for life. This feast is observed during the time of the wheat harvest, a major provision of the Lord. In Leviticus 23:15–16 God told the Jews: "You shall also count for yourselves from the day after the Sabbath, from the day when you brought in the sheaf of the wave offering; there shall be seven complete Sabbaths. You shall count fifty days to the day after the seventh Sabbath; then you shall present a new grain offering to the Lord."

A new grain offering was to be offered in the Feast of Weeks: "You shall bring in from your dwelling places two loaves of bread for a wave offering, made of two-tenths of an ephah; they shall be of a fine flour, baked with leaven as first-fruits to the Lord." Leaven is now introduced to the bread in place of the unleavened bread of the former feasts. But why? Checking with the messianic rabbis, I discovered a logical answer to this question. While the Passover is referring to God and the purging of sin, the Feast of Weeks or Pentecost refers to God's people who receive the law and the Spirit. We still have sin in our lives until we receive our new glorified bodies at the Rapture. We read in 1 Corinthians 10:17: "Since there is one bread, we who are many are one body; for we all partake of the one bread." The two loaves mentioned in Leviticus 23:17 picture the Jew and the Gentile, but we are now one body, "one loaf." There are a number of other offerings and sacrifices that are presented at the temple at this time as well, and they are applicable to several things, from sins to thanksgivings.

Counting of the Omer

According to Leviticus 23:15–16, the Jews were commanded to start counting fifty days from the day of the Feasts of Firstfruits to the next feast, the Feast of Weeks/Pentecost. During the forty-nine days of this count, which they call "the counting of the omer," the wheat crop is in the ripening process. By the end of the omer count, the crop is ready for harvest, and the firstfruits of the wheat crop can be brought to the temple for Pentecost on the fiftieth day. *Shavuot*, the Hebrew name for this festival, means "seven weeks." This concludes the festival season, which began at Passover. Just as Firstfruits celebrate the ripening of the barley crop, Shavuot celebrates the ripening of the wheat crop.

The Remembrances

The feasts all have a historical significance. The Feast of Passover is a remembrance of the slaying of the Passover Lamb. The first day of the Feast of Unleavened Bread is a remembrance of the exodus from Egypt. The Feast of Weeks is a remembrance of the giving of the law at Mount Sinai. The seventh day after Passover, according to tradition, reminds the Jews of the crossing of the Red Sea. The counting of the omer is regarded as a remembrance of the intervening days between the exodus from Egypt and the revelation at Sinai. That is why the Feast of Weeks became known as the anniversary of God's appearance at Mount Sinai.

On the first Feast of Weeks, signs and wonders accompanied the giving of the law. We read in Exodus 20:18: "All the people perceived the thunder and the lightning flashes and the sound of the trumpet and the mountain smoking; and when the people saw it, they trembled and stood at a distance." Thomas Lancaster, pastor of Beth Immanuel Sabbath Fellowship in Wisconsin, maintains that the Midrash also makes mention of what took place at the Feast of Weeks when the children of Israel heard the voice of God giving the law from Mt. Sinai. He says that according to the Midrash, a collection of Jewish oral traditions of the things that happened in history, the people in the camp saw sound waves in the form of fiery substances. Each commandment, as it left God's mouth, circled the whole camp and eventually rested on each Jew personally. He also noted from the Midrash that the people heard God's voice in many different languages.

Exodus 19:16 states: "So it came about on the third day, when it was morning, that there were thunder and lightning flashes and a thick cloud upon the mountain and a very loud trumpet sound, so that all the people who were in the camp trembled." The parallels are quite fascinating when we read Acts 2:2–6: "And suddenly there came from heaven a noise like a violent rushing wind, and it filled the whole house where they were sitting. And there appeared to them tongues as of fire distributing themselves, and they rested on each one of them. And they were all filled with the Holy Spirit and began to speak with other tongues, as the Spirit was giving them utterance. Now there were Jews living in Jerusalem, devout men from every nation under heaven. And when this sound occurred, the crowd came together, and were bewildered because each one of them was hearing them speak in his own language."

We cannot prove that everything recorded in the Midrash happened, but we can assume that all the people who were in the room in Acts 2 were familiar with the events. They could immediately make the connection between the Feast of Weeks and their present experience on the day of Pentecost as being of God.

Filling of the Spirit

The concept of the filling of the Spirit has always evoked different opinions regarding its meaning. One thing I observed about *filling* was that in the Greek there are two different words for the process. In Ephesians 5:18 the word for *filling* is *pleroo*, which conveys the idea of growth to maturity or being molded by the Word of God. If we compare Ephesians 5:18 to Colossians 3:16, which discusses the same subject, we can see that "be filled with the Spirit" is the same as "Let the word of Christ richly dwell within you." Since this command in Ephesians 5:18 is in the present tense, this indicates a continual experience or process. Both phrases have the same result: praise and thanksgiving to the Lord. On the other hand, *pimplemi* in Acts 2:4 is in the aorist tense, which indicates a single event or happening. In context, the word implies an empowering for a work of service. Today, since the Spirit indwells us as believers, we can be empowered by the Holy Spirit in our respective ministries. So the Holy Spirit is doing two major things for us: empowering and maturing us. It is also interesting to note that when Paul wrote in 1 Corinthians 6:19: "Or do you not know that your body is a temple of the Holy Spirit who is in you," he used the Greek word *naos*, which means "the innermost holy place of the Temple where God dwelt." The other word for temple, *hieron*, means "the entire temple." By Paul's use of the word *naos*, he wants believers to understand that their bodies are truly the intimate dwelling places of the Holy Spirit.

Further Observations

I was also intrigued by one important contrast between the Old Testament Feast of Weeks and the New Testament Feast of Pentecost. In Exodus 32:28, we find that three thousand men died on the day the law was given, but in Acts 2:41 we read that three thousand people were saved on the day the Holy Spirit was given. The law brought death, while the Spirit brought life!

It is interesting that the entire Godhead was involved in the fulfilling of the spring feasts. The *Son* honored and fulfilled the Feast of Passover by His death. The *Father* honored and fulfilled the Feast of Firstfruits by raising up Christ from death and the grave. The *Holy Spirit* honored and fulfilled the

Feast of Weeks/Pentecost by His descent fifty days after the resurrection of Christ. Now we, in response to the fulfilling work of the total Godhead, can truly serve the Lord in all power and truth!

Five

THE FEAST OF TRUMPETS

The First of the Fall Feasts

In studying and researching the historical and spiritual significances of the spring feasts and how Jesus fulfilled them, I was intrigued by how much God had revealed about His plans in these observances. While meditating and sorting out these discoveries, I began to look forward expectantly to what surprising facts lay ahead in studying the fall feasts. Since Jesus fulfilled the spring feasts by the events of His first coming, the parallels and the teachings became obvious. I wondered what truths could be gleaned from the fall feasts and how they could be understood, since Jesus has not yet fulfilled them.

As I began my study, I was pleased to discover that the fall feasts revealed incredible and exciting facts much like the spring feasts. Just as we have history to look to in the Scriptures for our understanding of the fulfilled feasts, we have prophecy in the Scriptures from which to draw to acquire an understanding of the unfulfilled feasts.

In understanding the practices and traditions of the fall feasts, I acquired a great deal of information from two rabbis: an orthodox rabbi, Shraga Simmons of Aish Ha Torah in Israel, and a messianic rabbi, Tzahi Shapira, the founder of Ahavat Ammi Ministries. From the information I gathered from these two rabbis, I began to observe fascinating pictures of God's prophetic plans concerning the second coming of the Messiah. In these remaining chapters I will attempt to unpack what appears to be the way Christ will fulfill these feasts.

Most Christians have probably never studied the Feast of Trumpets, because they might have considered it a Jewish feast with no application to believers today, especially to Gentiles. I have come to the opinion that it is time for Christians to give serious attention to the details of the biblical and traditional aspects of this mysterious feast.

We read in Leviticus 23:24: "Speak to the sons of Israel, saying, 'In the seventh month on the first of the month, you shall have a rest, a reminder by blowing of trumpets, a holy convocation.'" What is the purpose of this blowing of the trumpets, and what is this reminder? Since not as much is written in the Bible about this observance, I looked at the Jewish traditions to see if they would shed additional light on the subject. Again, I was astounded at what was revealed about Christ in those extra-biblical traditions!

To the Jews the most important aspect of this festival is that it is the Jewish New Year. It falls on the first day of Tishri, the seventh month of the sacred Hebrew lunar-solar calendar. It is also very significant in that it is the only feast that falls on the new moon, which I will explain later in this chapter. On this day, Jewish families enjoy the delicious tradition of eating slices of apples that have been dipped in honey. This is full of meaning to every Jew. They hope the year will be as sweet as the fruit they have eaten. I wondered why apples were chosen as the fruit. I found that the answer is rooted in the Talmud's understanding of Isaac's blessing of Jacob in Genesis 27:27, where Isaac said: "The smell of my son is like the smell of a field which the Lord has blessed." The Talmud identifies this field as an apple orchard. What a beautiful way to remember the biblical blessing that was bestowed on Jacob and all his descendants!

The Jews also refer to Rosh Hashanah, the Hebrew name for the Feast of Trumpets, by other names that have very interesting meanings. They are *Yom Teruah* (Day of Awakening Blast or Resurrection); *Yom Hadin* (Day of Judgment); *Yom Zikaron* (Day of Remembrance); and *Yom Hamelech* (Day of Coronation of the King). Interestingly, all the names allude to the coming of the Messiah. The trumpets are to announce His coming! The shofar is the trumpet used for this celebration. The shofar is blown to make an announcement or to proclaim what is coming. The Jews use two types of shofars. A small one is a ram's horn, and a larger Yemenite shofar comes from an African antelope called the kudu. One Sunday morning, I was on my way to church where I was to teach about the Feast of Trumpets. It occurred to me at the time that I should have borrowed a shofar from one of the local synagogues so I could show the people what one looked like. About thirty minutes before I was to speak, I happened to mention to a church member that I wished I had a shofar to show. To my complete surprise she excitedly informed me that she had a shofar in the trunk of her car! She had it because she was involved in some fundraising events for Israel, and had placed it in her trunk temporarily. It dawned on me that if God can provide the ram, He can certainly provide the ram's horn! Being a trumpet player, I couldn't resist demonstrating the blowing of the shofar. The sound was so loud that people in rooms across the hall started getting ready to get in single file for a fire drill. Fortunately, a potential panic was quickly dispelled!

The Shofar Blasts

I discovered that there were four types of blasts blown during the celebration. They are *Tekiah*, one long blast of alarm; *Shevarim*, three medium blasts like wailing; *Teruah*, nine short blasts like crying; and *Tekiah Hagedolah*, the longest and loudest blast. Let us take a look at each blast as the rabbis understand them.

First, the Tekiah, a three-second sustained note, is the sound of the king's coronation. Rosh Hashanah is the day of appreciating who God is. The Jews then internalize that understanding so that it becomes a living, practical part of everyday reality. In other words, God is all-powerful. God is the Creator. God is the Sustainer. God is the Supervisor. In short God is King of the universe. Rabbi Tzahi Shapira explains, "The word *Tekiah* really means 'to be stuck' or 'to stop or pause.' Hashem is getting our attention. God is trying to stop us and to focus on him." *Hashem* (literally in Hebrew, "the name") is the name Jews use for Yahweh, in order to avoid dishonoring His name. Also, Rabbi Shapira referred me to Psalm 46:10: "Cease striving and know that I am God; I will be exalted among the nations, I will be exalted in the earth."

Second, Shevarim—three medium wailing blasts—is the sobbing cry of a Jewish heart yearning to connect, to grow, to achieve. The Jew cries out to God from the depths of his soul. At this moment, his soul stands before the Almighty without any barriers, and he can truly let go. Rabbi Shapira said that shevarim means "to be broken" and is a sound of repentance in Hebrew. This is a time of asking for forgiveness.

Third, Teruah, nine quick blasts in short succession, resembles an alarm clock, arousing one from a spiritual slumber. The shofar brings clarity, alertness, and focus. The Jews say that on Rosh Hashanah they need to wake up and be honest and objective about their lives: who they are, where they've been, and in which direction they're headed. We must remember that this is the Jewish New Year, so they would obviously want to reassess their lives. Rabbi Shapira says, "Teruah, a series of short, staccato notes extending over a period of about three seconds, is a preparation to receive the king! Stand on guard; the king is about to arrive!"

Fourth, Tekiah Hagedolah, the final blast, a very long sound, is a call to come forth or to arise. It literally means the "Big Tekiah" and is the last trumpet of the service. It is the last call to repentance, before the great Day of the Lord. Rabbi Shapira also comments on this: "Tekiah Hagedolah is the final blast in a set, which lasts ten seconds minimum. This is the Tekiah that announces that the king has arrived (see 1 Thess. 4:16). We remember that Yeshua will arrive with a great Tekiah sound."

In this feast, there are one hundred different trumpet blasts blown with the belief that the gates of heaven will be opened for the home taking, which sounds like an allusion to the Rapture. The Tekiah and Tekiah Hagedolah are understood as sounds of triumph and joy, while the Shevarim and Teruah, in contrast, are sounds of pain, suffering, and repentance. The ceremonial blasts have a sequence that is followed exactly the same every time. It is in this order: *Tekiah, Shevarim-teruah, Tekiah*; *Tekiah, Shevarim, Tekiah*; *Tekiah, Teruah*, and then a final blast of *Tekiah Hagedolah* is held as long as possible. This arrangement makes thirty sounds for the series, with Tekiah being one note, Shevarim three, and Teruah nine. This grouping of thirty sounds is repeated twice more, making a total of ninety sounds. At the end of these three repetitions, a single formula of ten blasts closes the service, making a total of one hundred sounds altogether. This is to commemorate the one hundred cries of the mother of Sisera, the Canaanite general who did not make it home after being assassinated by Jael (Judg. 5:28). Apparently, this is to remind the Jews that no one can escape God's judgment for doing harm to His people.

Marji Hughes, a Jewish believer and director of Foundations Ministries in Missouri, made a very interesting application of the shofar. She said, "When the horn is removed from the ram, it is hollowed. The sound can only be produced when it is blown into. In the same way, we are told that Yeshua 'emptied himself' (Phil. 2:6–7). It was the Spirit moving through Yeshua, which enabled Him to produce the pure sound of the Father. We, too, are called to be shofars, as the Spirit of God moves through us. Unlike Yeshua, who emptied Himself, we are hollow by nature, empty of meaning until filled by the breath of God. By God's Spirit in us we become His voice, sounding forth the call to repentance as Matthew 10:20 says. "'For it is not you who speak, but it is the Spirit of your Father who speaks in you.'" What a beautiful application that is! In the celebration of the festival, the people recite Micah 7:18–20. After that, the congregations that are near a body of water will take stones with their sins written on them and cast them into the water. This activity helps them internalize what Micah says: "Yes, Thou wilt cast all their sins into the depths of the sea."

The Prophetic Implications

What are the prophetic implications of Rosh Hashanah? One of the names attached to the feast is Yom Zikaron, Day of

Remembrance. We read in Malachi 3:16–17: "Then those who feared the Lord spoke to one another, and the Lord gave attention and heard it, and a *book of remembrance* was written before Him for those who fear the Lord and who esteem His name. 'And they will be Mine,' says the Lord of hosts, 'on the day that I prepare *My own possession*, and I will *spare them* as a man spares his own son who serves him (emphasis mine).'" This seems to be saying that the Lord was eavesdropping on the believers and heard them honor Him. God then said that He would spare them as they were written in a book of remembrance.

From what would He spare them? The fourth chapter of Malachi describes the horrible time of judgment that will come on the whole earth, which is referred to in the book of Revelation as the Great Tribulation. We also read in Daniel 12:1: "Now at that time Michael, the great prince who stands guard over the sons of your people, will arise. And there will be a time of distress such as never occurred since there was a nation until that time; and at that time your people, everyone who is found written in the book, will be rescued." The rescued people are also called "My own possession," which means "peculiar treasure or wealth." This expression is used in several other passages of Scripture. We find it in Exodus 19:5: "Now then, if you will indeed obey My voice and keep My covenant, then you shall be *My own possession* (emphasis mine) among all the peoples, for all the earth is Mine." In Psalm 135:4 we read: "For the Lord has chosen Jacob for Himself, Israel for *His own possession* (emphasis mine)." And finally 1 Peter 2:9 says: "But you are a chosen race, a royal priesthood, a holy nation, a people for God's *own possession.*" The King James Version translates the description "a people for God's own possession" as "a peculiar people." I had always considered that expression as strange. But I discovered that the late Middle English word *peculiar* means "private property," and the root word of *peculiar* is the Latin word *pecus,* which means "cattle." In ancient cultures, one's net worth was described in terms of heads of cattle rather than dollars. That is why in Psalm 50:10 we are told that God owns all the cattle on a thousand hills. His wealth is immeasurable. Likewise, we are very valuable to God, so we are *pecu*liar to Him.

The Rapture

I discovered that quite a number of observations indicate that the Feast of Trumpets looks prophetically to the Rapture. Zola Levitt, the writer and teacher I met years ago, was the first one to direct me to them. Since the Rapture refers to the Church, many believers discount any association of this feast with the Rapture. They are of the opinion that the feasts in Leviticus pertain exclusively to Israel. True, the feasts have been given to the Jews, but God said emphatically that they were *His* feasts. The feasts are about Christ's agenda, not Israel's. We have already observed that the spring feasts are referring to all aspects of Christ's first coming: His death, burial, and resurrection. We also know that Pentecost refers to the coming of the Holy Spirit to indwell believers, the Church. Therefore, it logically follows that the fall feasts refer to the events surrounding Christ's second coming, which involves both Israel and the Church.

Several reasons make it apparent that the Feast of Trumpets does apply to the Rapture. One interesting point is that the longest gap between feasts is the gap between Pentecost and Trumpets. I believe that alludes to the lengthy time between Christ's two comings. There were months of silence from God between these two feasts without any new revelations, just like the interval between His two comings. Likewise, since Pentecost starts at varied times each year, the days between Pentecost and the Feast of Trumpets vary each year. But most importantly, as mentioned before, Rosh Hashanah (Feast of Trumpets) is the only feast that starts on the new moon. Why is that important? Because, according to the Talmud, the members of the Sanhedrin watched for the appearance of the new moon, because no one knew the day or hour when it would appear! Even today, Jews observe the feast for two days to make sure that they celebrate the feast on the exact day of the new moon, whichever day it would appear. (See Alfred Edersheim, *The Temple, Its Ministry and Services*, chapter 5.)

Also, a picture in the Jewish wedding custom is noteworthy. As discussed in an earlier chapter, after a prospective bride accepts the betrothal, the groom goes to prepare a chamber for his bride at his father's house. After the groom finishes preparing the bridal chamber, he must wait for his father to tell him when he can go take his bride. Of course, only the father knows when the proper time will be. In Mark 13:32 Jesus was quoting the typical response of a groom when asked when the wedding would take place. When His disciples asked when He would return, He answered, "But of that day or hour no one knows, not even the angels in heaven, nor the Son, but the Father alone." He was talking to His disciples as His future bride!

Now let's take another look at the two most quoted verses about the Rapture. In 1 Thessalonians 4:16–17, we read: "For the Lord Himself will descend from heaven with a shout, with the voice of the archangel, and *with the trumpet of God* (emphasis mine); and the dead in Christ will rise first. Then we who are alive and remain will be caught up together with them in the clouds to meet the Lord in the air, and so we shall always be with the Lord." Then 1 Corinthians 15:52 says: "In a moment, in the twinkling of an eye, at *the last trumpet* (emphasis mine); for the trumpet will sound, and the dead will be raised imperishable, and we will be changed." What is the last trumpet to which Paul is referring? It can't be the seventh trumpet of judgment in the book of Revelation, because that book had not been written yet. And the seventh trumpet in Revelation will be in the tribulation and will introduce the seven bowl judgments. No one asked Paul to which trumpet he was referring. They more than likely assumed that he was referring to the "Tekiah Hagedolah," the last of the one hundred trumpet blasts of Rosh Hashanah. It is also interesting to note that the groom did not enter the bride's dwelling. The bride would go out to meet him. Likewise, Christ will not come to our dwelling place, the earth, when He takes his bride at the Rapture. He will meet us in the air. In contrast to the Jewish bride bringing her personal belongings, all we will bring as the bride of Christ are the good works that we have done in our earthly life.

Since the spring feasts were fulfilled by Christ each on the exact day and hour, it would stand to reason that the fall feasts would also be fulfilled the same way. Imminency is still intact as a fundamental concept, since we still do not know the day or hour or even the year of the Rapture. But God never does anything at random. We might have misinterpreted Mark 13:32 in thinking that the Rapture could happen on any day of the year. The messianic Jews, with whom I have had the pleasure of discussing this concept, have all responded to me with this: "Of course the Rapture will happen at Rosh Hashanah!" Clearly the church age started at the Feast of Pentecost, and apparently it will end at the last trumpet blast of the Feast of Trumpets in the year God the Father has planned. We still do not know which day, hour, or year this event will occur. All we can do is follow the admonition of our Lord and Savior: "What I say to you I say to all, 'Be on the alert!'" (Mark 13:37). We watch by observing the signs of the times.

Six

THE DAY OF ATONEMENT

The Second of the Fall Feasts

The Day of Atonement (Yom Kippur) follows closely after Rosh Hashanah. We read in Leviticus 23: 26–28: "The Lord spoke to Moses, saying, 'On exactly the tenth day of this seventh month is the Day of Atonement; it shall be a holy convocation for you, and you shall humble your souls and present an offering by fire to the Lord. You shall not do any work on this same day, for it is a day of atonement, to make atonement on your behalf before the Lord your God.'" And Exodus 30:10 says: "And Aaron shall make atonement on its horns once a year; he shall make atonement on it with the blood of the sin offering of atonement once a year throughout your generations. It is most holy to the Lord."

The Jews consider the Day of Atonement the holiest day in all, for it is on this day that Israel would be forgiven of their sins or would face judgment. Devout Jews tell me that this day understandably brings plenty of anxiety into their hearts. Isn't it wonderful that we believers in our Lord and Savior Jesus Christ have the peace and assurance that our sins are forgiven eternally, because of what He has done on the cross! Yom Kippur literally means "Day of Covering." The word *Kippur* also means "ransom." It is to show God's willingness to cover the sins of the previous year. While the animal that was sacrificed had to be one year old in order to provide atonement for the previous sins for one year, Christ, being eternal, provided atonement for an eternity!

Leviticus 16:29 gives further instructions on how the Jews were to observe Yom Kippur: "On the tenth day of the seventh month *you shall humble your souls* and not do any work." In explaining what must characterize the act of humbling oneself, the rabbis say one must avoid eating and drinking, bathing or washing, marital relations, putting on perfumes or lotions, and wearing leather shoes. Now "refraining from the wearing of leather shoes" threw me. I asked about it and was informed that wearing leather shoes signified luxury. They wear comfort socks instead!

According to Leviticus 16:31–33, the high priest was to put on his linen garments and was to make atonement for the Most Holy Place, the tent or temple, the altar, himself (high priest), the priests (Levites), and the people (Israelites)—all in that order. Leviticus 16:3–4 states: "Aaron shall enter the holy place with this: with a bull for a sin offering and a ram for a burnt offering. He shall put on the holy linen tunic, and the linen undergarments shall be next to his body, and he shall be girded with the linen sash, and attired with the linen turban (these are holy garments). Then he shall bathe his body in water and put them on." This is not the colorful robe the high priest usually wore. This was a plain white linen garment. This observance was to be performed once a year according to Leviticus 16:34: "Now you shall have this as a permanent statute, to make atonement for the sons of Israel, for all their sins once every year." The procedure had four parts as spelled out in Leviticus 16:13–14: take fire from the altar of incense, offer sacrifices and place the blood of these sacrifices in a bowl, sprinkle the blood in the Holy Place and upon the mercy seat of the Ark seven times. The ingredients of the incense are found in Exodus 30:34: "Then the LORD said to Moses, 'Take for yourself spices, stacte and onycha and galbanum, spices with pure frankincense; there shall be an equal part of each.'"

The Scapegoat

One of the most important aspects of the observance of the Day of Atonement was the scapegoat. We read in Leviticus 16:7–8: "He shall take the two goats and present them before the Lord at the doorway of the tent of meeting. Aaron shall cast lots for the two goats, one lot for the Lord and the other lot for the scapegoat." Then verses 9–10 add: "Then Aaron shall offer the goat on which the lot for the Lord fell, and make it a sin offering. But the goat on which the lot for the scapegoat fell shall be presented alive before the Lord, to make atonement upon it, to send it into the wilderness as the scapegoat." Laying both hands on the head of the goat, the high priest then confessed the sins of the people. After that he sent the goat away to the wilderness by an appointed person. This fulfills the requirement explained in Leviticus 16:22: "The goat shall bear on itself all their iniquities to a solitary land; and he shall release the goat in the wilderness." This also ties into Isaiah 53:6, which says: "All of us like sheep have gone astray, each of us has turned to his own way; but the Lord has caused the iniquity of us all to fall on Him."

The Talmud, Tractate Shabbat Folio 86a, states: "How do we know that a crimson-colored strap is tied to the head of the goat that is sent [to 'Azaz'el]? Because it is said, 'If your sins be as scarlet, they shall be as white as snow (Isa. 1:18).' By a miracle this crimson-colored strap turned white, thus showing the people that they were forgiven of their sins." It then explains: "Rabbi Ishmael says, 'Now did they not have another sign? There was a crimson thread tied to the door of the sanctuary. When the goat had reached the wilderness, the thread would turn white, as it says, "Though your sins be as scarlet, they shall be white as snow."'"

That is fascinating, but this becomes totally amazing when another section of the Talmud (Yoma 39b) says: "Our Rabbis taught: 'During the last forty years before the destruction of the Temple the lot ['For the Lord'] did not come up in the right hand; nor did the crimson-colored strap become white ... and the doors of the Hekal (the temple) would open by themselves.'" After Christ was crucified, the crimson strap on the scapegoat and the crimson thread on the temple door never turned white again! Apparently, God was reminding the Jews that Jesus is the true scapegoat once and for all. Jesus fulfilled the promise of both goats. He paid the penalty for our sins and removed our sins as well! Since the lot that was drawn for the goat for sacrifice to the Lord never came up in the right hand, this, too, was a sign that God did not accept their offering again. Hebrews 9:11–12 says: "But when Christ appeared as a high priest of the good things to come, He entered through the greater and more perfect tabernacle, not made with hands, that is to say, not of this creation; and not through the blood of goats and calves, but through His own blood, He entered the holy place once for all, having obtained eternal redemption."

As already noted earlier, the Talmud says that the temple doors were found open by themselves each evening. In his writings, *The Wars of the Jews* (*Josephus Complete Works*), Josephus said, "At the same festival (Passover) . . . the Eastern gate of the inner court of the Temple, which was of brass, and vastly heavy, and had been with difficulty shut by twenty men, and rested upon a base armored with iron, and had bolts fastened very deep into the firm floor, which was there made of one entire stone, was seen to be opened of its own accord about the sixth hour of the night." This is similar to the tearing of the veil, which is a sign that there is now total access to God because of the redemptive work of Christ.

The Observances of Yom Kippur

According to Jewish tradition, the observance of Yom Kippur today consists of five services. They are (1) *Kol Nidre* (the evening service): confessional chant; (2) *Shacharit* (the early morning service): reading of Leviticus 16 in the temple; (3) *Musaf* (the second service): reading of the Day of Atonement; (4) *Mincha* (the afternoon service): reading of Jonah; (5) *Ne'ila* (the final service): closing or locking the books. I find it interesting that the book of Jonah is read, because Christ said that Jonah was a sign. We read in Luke 11:29–30: "As the crowds were increasing, He began to say, 'This generation is a wicked generation; it seeks for a sign, and yet no sign will be given to it but the sign of Jonah. For just as Jonah became a sign to the Ninevites, so will the Son of Man be to this generation.'"

Another tradition started when temple sacrifices were discontinued was the Kapparot, in which a devout Jewish man holds a white rooster by his right hand, swings it over his head three times, and recites: "This fowl shall be in my stead, shall be my atonement; it shall go to death, so that I can attain a good life and peace." This is so sad that their hearts yearn for forgiveness, yet many Jews have not yet found it in Jesus.

The Prophetic Implications

The heavenly events during the tribulation as described in the book of Revelation give the impression that Christ is acting out Yom Kippur. From my research, I have become aware that Jews traditionally believe that the Messiah will come on the day of Yom Kippur to cleanse and reestablish Israel. Michael Cory, the founder of Voice of Judah International Ministries in Lawrenceville, Georgia, explained it well: "Yom Kippur is the holiest, most solemn day of the year in Israel. According to the Talmud, it is the last day to repent and be forgiven as the heavenly court makes its final judgment on this day and the books are closed." The Book of Revelation reveals that several things are going on in heaven while the Tribulation is occurring on earth. These events in heaven are described with images such as the golden censer and incense, and the robe dipped in blood. These images remind us of the procedures employed by the high priest in the performance of his duties in the Temple during Yom Kippur.

William Barclay discusses the details of the activities of the high priest during the Day of Atonement in his exposition of Hebrews 9:6–10 in his Daily Study Bible. In Barclay's words: "The high priest took coals from the altar and put them in a censer; he took incense and put it in a special dish; and then he walked into the Holy of Holies to burn incense in the very presence of God. It was laid down that he must not stay too long 'lest he put Israel in terror.' The people literally watched with bated breath; and when he came out from the presence of God still alive, there went up a sigh of relief like a gust of wind." Barclay did a good job of describing the emotions of the people at that moment. Their relief might have been not only for the priest when he emerged, but also for the forgiveness of their sins for yet another year.

When Jesus, their heavenly High Priest, comes down out of the heavenly temple, the people of Israel will display a different emotion. We read in Zechariah 12:10: "I will pour out on the house of David and on the inhabitants of Jerusalem, the Spirit of grace and of supplication, so that they will look on Me whom they have pierced; and they will mourn for Him, as one mourns for an only son, and they will weep bitterly over Him like the bitter weeping over a firstborn." Instead of a temporary forgiveness, they will receive an eternal forgiveness! Romans 11:26–27 promises: "And so all Israel will be saved, as it is written: 'The Deliverer will come from Zion, He will remove ungodliness from Jacob. This is My covenant with them, when I take away their sins.'"

It is also important to note another contrast between the earthly high priest and Jesus, their heavenly High Priest. The blood on the robe of the earthly high priest was from the animal sacrifice that provided ceremonial cleansing, while the blood on the robe of the heavenly High Priest recorded in Revelation 19:13 is from His enemies when He comes to cleanse the land as the Messiah. In other words, instead of a mere ceremonial cleansing, Jesus as the High Priest and Messiah does an actual overt cleansing of the land. This is explained in Isaiah 63:1–4: "Who is this who comes from Edom, with garments of glowing colors from Bozrah, this One who is majestic in His apparel, marching in the greatness of His strength? 'It is I who speak in righteousness, mighty to save.' Why is Your apparel red, and Your garments like the one who treads in the wine press? 'I have trodden the wine trough alone, and from the peoples there was no man with Me. I also trod them in My anger and trampled them in My wrath; and their lifeblood is sprinkled on My garments, and I stained all My raiment. For the day of vengeance was in My heart, and My year of redemption has come.'" Therefore, looking at both Jewish tradition and the Scriptures, it appears that Jesus the High Priest and Messiah will come out of the heavenly temple to earth at Yom Kippur, His second coming, administering judgment to unbelievers still alive as well as salvation to those believers still alive at the end of the Tribulation.

The correlation between the first two fall feasts, Rosh Hashanah and Yom Kippur, is startling. The feast days of Rosh Hashanah and Yom Kippur, along with the seven days in between, are known collectively as "the Days of Awe." In other words, two days of Rosh Hashanah plus seven additional Days of Awe, totaling nine days, makes the next day, the tenth day, Yom Kippur. As the Jews understand the seven days between the feasts as a time of judgment and a time to avoid the trappings of the world, believers understand that the seven years in heaven after the Rapture will be a time of judgment away from the trappings of this world as well. I am referring to the judgment seat of Christ, when we will be judged according to our deeds, whether worthy or unworthy. In 2 Corinthians 5:10, we read: "For we must all appear before the judgment seat of Christ, so that each one may be recompensed for his deeds in the body, according to what he has done, whether good or bad." This paints a great picture of the future when we as believers will be in heaven with our High Priest, Jesus Christ, for seven years receiving our rewards.

Also another picture is seen in the custom of the Jewish wedding. When the groom brings his bride to the bridal chamber, which he prepared for her in his father's house, they celebrate their union for seven days before the wedding feast. We, as His bride, will be with Christ, our bridegroom, for seven years at the place He has prepared for us at His Father's house. After those seven years, we will return with our Lord at His second coming as He administers judgment to unbelievers on the earth and salvation to believing Israel, thereby fulfilling Yom Kippur just as the earthly high priest did! Interestingly, the Jews expect the Messiah will come at Yom Kippur to administer judgment or forgiveness. "And I saw heaven opened; and behold, a white horse, and He who sat upon it is called Faithful and True; and in righteousness He judges and wages war. His eyes are a flame of fire, and upon His head are many diadems; and He has a name written upon Him which no one knows except Himself. He is clothed with a robe dipped in blood; and His name is called The Word of God. And the armies which are in heaven, clothed in fine linen, white and clean, were following Him on white horses" (Rev. 19:11–14).

The judgment which Jesus brings to earth in fulfillment of Yom Kippur are explained in the next verse of the same chapter, "And from His mouth comes a sharp sword, so that with it He may smite the nations; and He will rule them with a rod of iron; and He treads the wine press of the fierce wrath of God, the Almighty. And on His robe and on His thigh He has a name written, 'King of Kings, and Lord of Lords.'" As noted earlier in Zechariah 12:10, Jesus the Messiah will also bring salvation to believing Jews. Their eyes will be opened to the truth about Jesus, when He returns!

In the first chapter we saw that the Jews expect the Messiah to come at Passover to bring redemption. On the other hand, they talk about the Messiah coming and bringing judgment or forgiveness at Yom Kippur. Isn't it amazing that in the observances of the feasts, the concept of both the first and second coming of the Messiah is embedded in their celebrations!

I came across this heartbreaking quote from Rabbi Yochanan Ben-Zakkai of the Yavneh Council. The Yavneh Council was the council of rabbis that determined the procedures to be followed after the temple was destroyed so traditions would still be intact for future generations. He said in the Talmud in *Berakoth 28b*: "Now I am being led before the Supreme King of Kings, the Holy One, blessed be He, who lives and endures for ever and ever. If He is angry with me, He is angry forever. If He puts me to death, He puts me to death forever. I cannot persuade Him with words or bribe Him with money. Moreover, there are two ways ahead of me: one leads to paradise and the other to hell, and I do not know which one will take me. How can I do anything but weep?"

How incredibly heart-wrenching that is! This must be the inner cry of every devout Jew if they have not as of yet found forgiveness and peace in Jesus their Messiah.

Seven

THE FEAST OF TABERNACLES

The Third of the Fall Feasts

The Feast of Tabernacles, the last of the fall feasts, is just as amazing as the others. Since I was so overwhelmed at how much information God placed in the traditions of the Rosh Hashanah and Yom Kippur, I should not have been surprised that this feast is likewise immensely full of insights about God's plans. But I must confess that I was just as overcome by my amazement at the magnitude of what God revealed in this fascinating festival because like the other feasts, this one, too, has prophetic implications as well as historical and spiritual significance. The Hebrew word for the feast is *sukkot*, which means "booths."

We are first introduced to the Feast of Tabernacles or Booths in Leviticus 23:33–36, which says: "Again the Lord spoke to Moses, saying, 'Speak to the sons of Israel, saying,

"On the fifteenth of this seventh month is the Feast of Booths for seven days to the Lord. On the first day is a holy convocation; you shall do no laborious work of any kind. For seven days you shall present an offering by fire to the Lord."" This seventh feast, Sukkot, given to Israel is observed from the fifteenth to the twenty-second of Tishri. During this time, many Jewish families construct a *sukkah*, a hastily built hut in which meals are eaten throughout the festival. The sukkah was used to help the people remember the huts Israel lived in during their forty years in the wilderness after their exodus from Egypt. In time they developed a custom of decorating the huts or booths with hanging fruits and other ornaments. It is interesting that America possibly celebrated Sukkot in its early history as many Jews have surmised. In 1621, when the pilgrims gathered to give thanks to the Lord for their first fall harvest, it is understood that they actually celebrated Sukkot, or used it as a model for the celebration of thanks to the Lord for the harvest. This eventually became the holiday of Thanksgiving in 1863.

For forty days from the first of Elul to the tenth of Tishri of the Hebrew calendar, Moses stayed on Mount Sinai a second time. Jews consider this a time for repentance and call it *Teshuvah*. When Moses descended the mountain with God's command to build a tabernacle, the people began to build it with explicit instructions found in Exodus 35–40. The tabernacle is, in reality, God's Sukkah! Just as the Hebrew children gathered materials for building the tabernacle as commanded, in the same way, the Jews of our time also start preparing for Sukkot building their sukkah right after they finish observing Yom Kippur.

The Concept of Joy

In contrast to Yom Kippur, the Feast of Tabernacles is a season of great joy. In fact, *joy* is a predominant feature of the feast. The people were to be joyful for all that God had provided for them from the harvests of grain and fruit. The Passover, Pentecost, and Tabernacles are often referred to as the pilgrim feasts, because all the males each year were to appear before the Lord in the place where God chose, according to Deuteronomy 16:16–17. At the Passover, though, *joy* is not mentioned, and the word *joy* occurs only once in the instructions for the Feast of Pentecost. However, when we come to Sukkot, *joy* is mentioned twice. In Deuteronomy 16:13–15 we read: "You shall celebrate the Feast of Booths seven days after you have gathered in from your threshing floor and your wine vat; and you shall rejoice in your feast . . . because the Lord your God will bless you in all your produce and in all the work of your hands, so that you shall be altogether joyful." This all makes sense when we look at these three feasts from the agricultural perspective. Passover is the planting season; Pentecost is the wheat harvesttime; and the Feast of Tabernacles is when the fruit is harvested. When all the harvest seasons were complete, there was much rejoicing, and the feast was also called the Feast of Ingathering. When we look at the Feast of Tabernacles, from the spiritual perspective, we can see that it has three purposes for the people. First, it brought joy that their sins were forgiven (during Yom Kippur). Second, it reminded them of God's provision and presence during the Exodus. Third, it reminded them that God was still present and provided for all their needs. Also, it should be noted that in Nehemiah 8, the Israelites celebrated the Feast of Tabernacles for the first time since the days of Joshua. Ezra, the scribe, read from the book of the law of God each day during the celebration. What a reminder it is that when we as believers worship together, the Word of God is to be the center focus!

The Traditions of the Building of the Sukkah

God gave the Jews three key instructions for celebrating Sukkot. We find the first instruction in Leviticus 23:40: "Now on the first day you shall take for yourselves the foliage of beautiful trees, palm branches and boughs of leafy trees and willows of the brook; and you shall rejoice before the Lord your God for seven days." They are to gather four different plant materials. We see the second instruction in Leviticus 23:42: "You shall live in booths for seven days; all the native-born in Israel shall live in booths." They were to live in a hut, or *sukkah*. The third instruction is found in Deuteronomy 16:13–14: "You shall celebrate the Feast of Booths seven days after you have gathered in from your threshing floor and your wine vat; and you shall rejoice in your feast, you and your son and your daughter and your male and female servants and the Levite and the stranger and the orphan and the widow who are in your towns." They were to rejoice before the Lord.

The rabbis of our day have added some more instructions for the construction of the sukkah. I have found eight instructions described by John Parsons, a teacher and author on Jewish topics:

1. The sukkah must have nothing hanging above it, such as branches of a tree.
2. There should be sufficient space to sit at a table.
3. It should be made of sturdy-enough material to withstand wind.
4. The top must be made of plant or tree material.
5. At night the stars must be visible through the roof, with ample shade in the day.
6. Ceiling decorations are permissible including flowers, hanging fruits, ornaments, or similar items.
7. Jewish-related posters or pictures can be hung on the walls.
8. Decorating the outside with Christmas lights is permissible.

The Ceremony of the Festival

When Jews today celebrate the Feast of Tabernacles, they recite a blessing on the first night, and then they light two candles. The blessing is this: "Sanctify us, Lord our God, King of the universe, who blessed the holiday of light to kindle and command us with His mitzvoth. Blessed are You, Lord our God, King of the universe, for keeping us alive, taking care of us, and bringing us to this time."

According to the *Encyclopedia Britannica*, a *mitzvoth* is "any commandment, ordinance, law, or statute contained in the Torah (first five books of the Bible) and, for that reason, to be observed by all practicing Jews." Each evening before the main meal, the Jews would recite the *kiddush*, a blessing related to sanctification: "Sanctify us, Lord our God, King of the universe, who blessed us to dwell in the sukkah, and commanded us with His mitzvoth." Traditionally, the meal includes stuffed cabbage dishes and fruit or fresh vegetable turnovers. The host of the celebration invites imaginary guests to the meal. Abraham is invited to attend the first night, and then Isaac, Jacob, Joseph, Moses, Aaron, and King David are invited the following nights. Another aspect of the observance is the waving of what is called a *lulav*. This is a bouquet that is made from palm, myrtle, and willow branches and bound together so it can be waved in praise of the Lord. The instructions are to first bind the branches together—two willows on the left, one palm branch in the center, and three myrtles on the right. Next, the bundle is to be held in the right hand. In the left hand they are to hold an *etrog*, a lemon-like citrus fruit (pointing downward) and to lift them together while reciting the blessing, "Blessed are You, Lord our God, King of the universe, for keeping us alive, taking care of us, and bringing us to this time." While they recite the blessing, they are then to turn the etrog right side up, and, with both hands side by side, shake the lulav three times in each direction: front, right, back, left, up, and down. These six directions indicate the all-encompassing presence of God.

The etrog, branches of palm trees, myrtle, and willows of the brook are the four plant materials that the Jews use to comply with the instructions in Leviticus 23:40. I asked several sources what might be the reasons for their using these four things. The most feasible reasons I found were as follows: the palm branches reminded them of the valleys and plains; the boughs of trees reminded them of the bushes on the mountain heights; the willows reminded them of the brooks; and the etrog reminded them of the fruits of the land God gave them. The lulav is also shaken during the reading of the praise psalms in the morning service. A hymn that asks to "save us" is also sung. When the weekly Sabbath arrives, Ecclesiastes is read. Possibly this was to remind the Jews that life makes sense only when one trusts the Lord. Psalm 118:15 might refer to this festival when it says: "The sound of joyful shouting and salvation is in the tents of the righteous."

Ceremonies of the Temple

When the temple was still present in Jerusalem, the ceremonies that were a part of the Feast of Tabernacles were quite elaborate, according to Jewish historians such as Alfred Edersheim (See *The Temple, its Ministry and Services*, chapter 14). The ceremonies involved water and light, which symbolized various aspects of the presence of God.

Water-Pouring Ceremony

At the temple the high priest would draw water from the Pool of Siloam in a golden pitcher. He would then bring it through the water gate and pour it into a silver basin at the altar. The people would wave their *lulavot* (plural for *lulav*) and sing, "Save now, I pray, O Lord; O Lord, I pray, send now prosperity." During this water ceremony, the high priest would recite Isaiah 12:1–2: "Then you will say on that day, 'I will give thanks to you, O Lord; For although you were angry with me, Your anger is turned away, and You comfort me. Behold, God is my salvation. I will trust and not be afraid; For the Lord God is my strength and song. And He has become my salvation.'" The golden pitcher symbolizes the glory of God, while silver represents purity and righteousness, which can come only from God's salvation and refining of His people. Water, in this context, illustrates the outpouring of the Holy Spirit. Isaiah 12:3 says, "Therefore you will joyously draw water from the springs of salvation." Interestingly, the word translated as *salvation* here is the word *yeshua*, the same Hebrew word for the name of Jesus. Ezekiel 36:25 makes a clear promise about salvation, using water figuratively: "I will sprinkle clean water on you, and you will be clean."

The rabbis taught that this water-drawing ceremony was more than simply a request for winter rains. It was to illustrate the days of messianic redemption when the waters of the Holy Spirit will be poured out on all Israel (Sukkoth 55). In John 7:37–38, we read about how Jesus responded to this feast in His ministry: "Now on the last day, the great day of the feast, Jesus stood and cried out, saying, 'If anyone is thirsty, let him come to Me and drink. He who believes in Me, as the Scripture said, "From his innermost being will flow rivers of living waters."'"

In the next verse, John explains what Jesus was referring to: "But this He spoke of the Spirit, whom those who believed in Him were to receive; for the Spirit was not yet given, because Jesus was not yet glorified." The Holy Spirit allows us to experience Immanuel, "God with us." But many of the people did not appreciate the words Jesus spoke. The leaders were quite upset when the temple guards refused their order to arrest Jesus. When one of their own, Nicodemus, spoke in Jesus' defense, they responded by saying, "No prophet arises out of Galilee" (John 7:52). They conveniently ignored Isaiah 9:1–2, which says: "He shall make it glorious, by the way of the sea, on the other side of Jordan, *Galilee* (emphasis mine) of the Gentiles. The people who walk in darkness will see a great light; those who live in a dark land, the light will shine on them." Even today though the Middle East is dark spiritually, the light of the gospel is still shining!

The Light Show

After the water ceremony, during the evening, four seventy-five-foot-tall menorahs were lit up. The priests would put on a light show all night with torch dances, while the Levites sang and played music. As a result, the Feast of Tabernacles

was often referred to as the "Show of Lights." The Babylonian
Talmud quotes a rabbi who referred to the light show by saying, "He who has not seen the rejoicing at the show has never
seen rejoicing in his life" (Sukkah 5:1). And that brings us to
the second Sukkot symbol—light—that Jesus used to point
to Himself as the fulfillment of Scripture. God had promised
in Isaiah 9:1–2 that a great light would shine out of Galilee.
In John 8:12, Jesus said, "I am the light of the world; he who
follows Me will not walk in the darkness, but will have the
light of life."

In John 7:1–9, we read that Jesus' brothers wanted Him to
go up to Judea with them to celebrate the Feast of Tabernacles.
Jesus responded, "My time is not yet here, but your time is
always opportune. The world cannot hate you; but it hates
Me because I testify of it, that its deeds are evil. Go up to
the feast yourselves; I do not go up to this feast because My
time has not yet fully come." As discussed in an earlier chapter, Jesus would not do anything openly in relationship to the
feasts unless He was fulfilling something. I will make some
observations concerning the prophetic implications of Sukkot.
But first I want to make some comments about Jesus' birth in
relation to this feast.

Jesus' Birth and Sukkot

Strong evidence seems to suggest that Jesus was actually
born during the Feast of Tabernacles. First, at the time of

His birth, lambs and shepherds were in the field. That probably would not have been the case if the season was during the winter months. Second, three of the festivals, as noted earlier, were called "pilgrimage" festivals. The reason there was no room at the inn for Joseph and Mary was that everyone was heading to Jerusalem apparently to celebrate one of those feasts. This might be why the Romans took advantage of the time to take a census. All accommodations in Bethlehem, a few miles away, also would have been booked up with travelers. Third, John the Baptist was conceived right after his father Zacharias, who was a priest, was serving in the temple. We know when Zacharias was serving in the temple because we know what priestly order he served in, which was *Abiyah*. 1 Chronicles 24:7–18, as well as the Talmud, tells us when each of the twenty-four orders of priests would serve in the temple, and for how long. Each order of priests served for one week and during the weeks of the pilgrimage feasts. Each one of the twenty-four orders of priests would begin and end its service in the Temple on the Sabbath, according to 2 Chronicles 23:8. Starting with the month of Nisan (first month of the Hebrew calendar), we can figure that Zacharias was serving the tenth week of the year, because he had the eighth cycle of temple service as well as the Feast of Unleavened Bread and the Feast of Pentecost. That would mean that John the Baptist probably was conceived about the third week of Sivan, when Zacharias returned home.

Luke 1 states that Jesus was conceived by the Holy Spirit

six months after Elizabeth became pregnant. Thus Jesus would have been born six months after John. Assuming the usual forty-week term of pregnancy, John, whom Jesus referred to as "The Elijah who was to come before the Messiah," would have been born during Passover. Counting the weeks from the latter part of Sivan, we arrive at the middle of Nisan, the time of the Passover. The Jews believed that Elijah would come on the Passover. This is why they have a place and a cup for Elijah at the Seder dinner. We read about Jesus' teaching about John the Baptist in Matthew 17:10–13: "And His disciples asked Him: 'Why then do the scribes say that Elijah must come first?' And He answered and said, 'Elijah is coming and will restore all things; but I say to you, that Elijah already came, and they did not recognize him, but did to him whatever they wished. So also the Son of Man is going to suffer at their hands.' Then the disciples understood that He had spoken to them about John the Baptist." Now if we count six months from John's birth, we come to the middle of Tishri, the Feast of Tabernacles! Also of interest is the possibility that Jesus might have been conceived on Hanukkah, the festival of lights, by counting back forty weeks from the Feast of Tabernacles. Therefore, He apparently was conceived on the "festival of lights" and born during the "show of lights," the Feast of Tabernacles. With these two events as bookends, what an appropriate statement Jesus made when He said, "I am the light of the world; he who follows Me will not walk in darkness, but will have the light of life" (John 8:12).

The Prophetical Implications of Sukkot

In Jeremiah 23:7–8, the Lord promised: "'Therefore behold, the days are coming,' declares the Lord, 'when they will no longer say, "As the Lord lives, who brought up the sons of Israel from the land of Egypt," but, "As the Lord lives, who brought up and led back the descendants of the household of Israel from the north land and from all the countries where I had driven them." Then they will live on their own soil.'" Ezekiel shed more light when he prophesied in Ezekiel 37:26–28: "And I will make a covenant of peace with them; it will be an ever-lasting covenant with them. And I will place them and multiply them, and will set My sanctuary in their midst forever. My dwelling place also will be with them; and I will be their God, and they will be My people. And the nations will know that I am the Lord who sanctifies Israel, when My sanctuary is in their midst forever."

The Lord will dwell with His people forever! He will "tab-ernacle" with us! We will observe the Feast of Tabernacles every year in the kingdom to celebrate this fact. The prophet Zechariah prophesied by saying: "Then it will come about that any who are left of all the nations that went against Jerusalem will go up from year to year to worship the King, the Lord of hosts, and to celebrate the Feast of Booths. And it will be that whichever of the families of the earth does not go up to Jerusalem to worship the king, the Lord of hosts, there will be no rain on them" (Zech. 14:16–17). I would venture to say, my fellow Texans will all show up because they know what it's like to have no rain! While noting that the Feast of Tabernacles looks to the millennial kingdom, I wondered why the feast was five days after Yom Kippur. Was there any significance to the five days? Remember, we discussed earlier that the number five in Hebraic numerology stands for *grace*. It is definitely God's grace when He comes to set up His kingdom on earth to live and reign with us!

Shemini Atzeret (Eighth Day)

Of interest is the fact that eight days are included in this seven-day feast! At the end of the Feast of Tabernacles, the Jews were instructed in Numbers 29:35: "On the eighth day you shall have a solemn assembly; you shall do no laborious work." The Babylonian Talmud explains in Sukkah 55b that during the festival of Sukkoth seventy bulls were sacrificed for the seventy nations at the time of the temple, but on the eighth day, Shemini Atzeret, only one bull was sacrificed for Israel alone. Atzeret comes from the Hebrew root, *atzar*, meaning "to hold back or stop." On the eighth day, the Jews would stop and pray for rain for the future harvests, but it also was a more intimate time with the Lord. The number eight has often carried the symbolic meaning of "new beginning." Since the Feast of Tabernacles celebrates the millennial reign of the Lord, the eighth day, being a convocation of its own, looks toward fellowship with God for eternity and a new beginning. Revelation 21:1–2 says: "Then I saw a new heaven and a new earth; for the first heaven and the first earth passed away, and there is no longer any sea. And I saw the holy city, new Jerusalem, coming down out of heaven from God, made ready as a bride adorned for her husband." And the following verse continues: "And I heard a loud voice from the throne, saying, 'Behold, the tabernacle of God is among men, and He shall dwell among them, and they shall be His people, and God Himself shall be among them.'"

CONCLUSION

We can see now that God was very careful to inform us of His plans for Christ's intervention in the history of mankind. Because of our ability to see what happened in recorded history about Christ's first coming, we can marvel at how explicitly He fulfilled the pictures displayed in the spring feasts from Passover to Pentecost. Because of the prophecies that God so graciously gave us in the Scriptures, we can also understand how explicitly He plans to fulfill the pictures displayed about His second coming in the fall feasts from the Feast of Trumpets to the Feast of Tabernacles. God's pictures, parallels, and cycles are so impressive that it would seem that anyone who observed them would come to faith in Jesus Christ as his Savior and Messiah. Since many do not respond that way, this shows that the ministry of the Holy

Spirit is necessary to bring a person to put his trust in Jesus.

For us who have a relationship with our Savior, we can learn some very important spiritual lessons from the feasts in relation to our walk with Him. The first three spring feasts teach us to walk with an attitude of gratitude, because of what Jesus did. Furthermore, the Feast of Pentecost teaches us to walk with an attitude of dependence, because of what the Holy Spirit is doing. And finally, the fall feasts teach us to walk with an attitude of expectancy, because of what Jesus will do.

The Pictures from the Harvests

In review, it is very interesting that God apparently patterned the order of resurrections after the patterns of the harvests. The rapture of the church can be illustrated by the barley harvest because of the winnowing by the wind, the softness of the shell, and its being in the first harvest season. Those believers who come out of the tribulation are illustrated by the wheat harvest because of the stiff upright neck and the crushing by the tribulum. The taking away of unbelievers for impending judgment at the end of the Tribulation in the Battle of Armageddon is illustrated by the fruit harvest and the winepress. And the ushering of the surviving believers out of the Tribulation is illustrated by the gleanings because they are not harvested or resurrected but they live on in the Millennium in their non-resurrected bodies.

Christ's Fulfillment of the Feasts

As for the spring feasts, Christ has fulfilled each one on the very day of the feasts, as I previously noted. Christ honored and fulfilled the Passover by His death. He honored and fulfilled the Feast of Unleavened Bread by His burial. Christ honored and fulfilled the Feast of Firstfruits by His resurrection from the grave. Christ honored and fulfilled the Feast of Pentecost by sending the Holy Spirit fifty days after His resurrection.

As for the fall feasts, Christ will honor and fulfill the Feast of Trumpets by taking His bride to the Father's house. Christ will honor and fulfill the Day of Atonement by His second advent. He will honor and fulfill the Feast of Tabernacles by His setting up of the kingdom on earth and dwelling with us. Christ may well fulfill the fall feasts on the exact days of each of the feasts, just as He did on the spring feasts.

Our Response

Time is short, and the time of the fulfillment of the fall feasts by Christ's second coming is close upon us. In light of these teachings from the Scriptures, what should be our response? The apostle Peter answered this question eloquently under God's inspiration with four major points in 2 Peter 3:14–18: "Therefore, beloved, since you look for these things, *be diligent* to be found by Him in peace, spotless and blameless, and *regard the patience* of our Lord to be salvation; just as also our beloved brother Paul, according to the wisdom given him, wrote to you, as also in all his letters, speaking in them of these things, in which are some things hard to understand, which the untaught and unstable distort, as they do also the rest of the Scriptures, to their own destruction. You therefore, beloved, knowing this beforehand, *be on your guard* so that you are not carried away by the error of unprincipled men, and fall from your own steadfastness, but *grow in the grace and knowledge* of our Lord and Savior Jesus Christ. To Him be the glory, both now and to the day of eternity. Amen (all emphasis mine)"

The main thing to remember as we see God's program unfolding for us in His intervention in the history of mankind is these loving words Christ spoke in John 15:15: "No longer do I call you slaves, for the slave does not know what his master is doing; but I have called you friends, for all things that I have heard from My Father I have made known to you."

BIBLIOGRAPHY

Babylonian Talmud, The, Hebrew-English Edition, *Berakoth 28b*. London: Soncino Press, 1984.

Barclay, William, "The Letter to the Hebrews," from his *Daily Bible Study* series, revised edition. Louisville, KY: Westminster John Knox Press, 1976.

Edersheim, Alfred, *The Temple: Its Ministry and Services*. Grand Rapids, MI: WM. B. Eerdmans Publishing Company, 1975.

Encyclopedia Britannica, 15th Edition, Volume 8. Chicago, IL: University of Chicago, 1993.

Hoehner, Harold W., Chronological Aspects of the Life of Christ Part VI, "Daniel's Seventy Weeks and New Testament Chronology," *Bibliotheca Sacra*, Vol. 132, January-March 1975.

Josephus, Flavius, *Josephus Complete Works*. Edition is a combination of the William Whiston translation published by William P. Nimmo, Edinburgh, Scotland, 1867, and the Standard Edition published by Porter and Coates, Philadelphia, PA. "A Harmony of the Numbering Systems in the Greek and English editions of the Works of Flavius Josephus" was added in 1978 by Neal Windham. Grand Rapids, MI: Kregel Publications, 1980.

Keil, C. F. and F. Delitzsch, *Biblical Commentary on the Old Testament*. Volume I. Translated from German by Rev. James Martin, B.A. Grand Rapids, MI: WM. B. Eerdmans Publishing Co., 1971.

Tabory, Joseph, "The Crucifixion of the Paschal Lamb," *Jewish Quarterly Review*, New Series, Volume 86, January-April 1996. Philadelphia, PA: University of Pennsylvania Press.

ABOUT THE
AUTHOR

Michael Norten received a ThM from Dallas Theological Seminary in 1974. He has served on the staff of Campus Crusade for Christ and as a Bible instructor, representing various ministries for more than forty years. He was an associate pastor of Lewisville Bible Church in Lewisville, Texas, and served as interim pastor and pulpit supply for a number of churches in North Texas. He has been an independent representative and regional vice president of a financial services company for thirty years. He resides in Dallas, Texas, with his wife, Ann.